# What others Are Saying About Our Books…

*ISP® Certification The Industrial Security Professional Exam Manual*
"Written by a security consultant with twenty-two years of experience in military intelligence, contracting and security, ISP Certification: The Industrial Security Professional Exam Manual is an instructional resource created to provide career security specialists with what they need to know to protect our nation's secrets. The text offers practical advice for security professionals and a working understanding of the NISPOM and Presidential Executive Orders implementing the National Industrial Security Program, but the heart of ISP Certification is its four practice tests designed to probe the depths of one's knowledge. An absolute "must-have" for anyone in federal positions requiring a thorough knowledge of security procedures, and highly recommended for the libraries of federal agencies." Midwest Book Review

"Right on target! Jeffrey Bennett's exam manual is the perfect supplement to the NISPOM for anyone preparing to take the Industrial Security Professional certification exam. The approach is clear and easy to use. It's definitely worth the price and more." William H. Henderson, author, Security Clearance Manual

"After receiving this book, I quickly skimmed through it prior to sitting down for a close study. My initial reaction was to wonder just how much information I could learn based on the fact that most of the book was dedicated to practice tests. When I finally took the time to sit down and read it, I was surprised at just how much information it contains. The book tells you how to prepare, to include learning all security disciplines, how to manage your time, and how to study the NISPOM. The practice tests are a great opportunity to time yourself, and help to identify areas of weakness. I truly recommend this book for anyone considering the ISP Certification… it is a great tool to have!"

"As most others I am a seasoned FSO. However, based on research I did, once I decided to take the ISP Exam I quickly learned to not take it cold. I got my workbook from NCMS and researched what other tools are out there to better help prepare me for the exam. I quickly discovered Mr. Bennett's ISP certification manual and after reading the overwhelmingly positive reviews I knew this would be well worth the money! "

"I've ordered a few of your products, to include the ISP manual and flash cards. I wanted you to know that I took the ISP exam this morning and passed! Your products were very helpful."

"I could not have attained a high score on the ISP exam without your study materials. The study materials you provided helped me prepare for this certification. I am very happy to be a part of this elite group of professionals."

"I could not have attained a high score on the ISP exam without your study materials. The study materials you provided helped me prepare for this certification. I am very happy to be a part of this elite group of professionals." Tony Cirafice, ISP Security Specialist

"The study guide has helped keep me up to date on the NISPOM." Kenneth Chaney, ISP, GA

"You have captivated the reader's interest!! Throughout the reading, you continue to address educational encouragement, experience and networking. The emphasis on mentoring just goes to show you how important it is to have support of your peers. Many who may be apprehensive about taking the exam, probably feel like they are all alone and no one is there to lean on. This book is an amazing tool to help guide and support those interested in rising to the next level. This book supports the certification's demonstration of willingness for self-improvement and dedication to the profession." Deb Jaramillo, ASIS North AL Chapter Secretary

"As a seasoned security professional, I found the Industrial Security Professional Exam Manual to be very clear, brief and concise. The ISP manual is a must read for anyone anticipating taking the ISP exam. Whether you are a seasoned security professional or a newbie to the world of security, this book is a keeper. Thank you for putting out such a Great Book ." Diane Griffin, President/CEO, Security First & Associates LLC

"Like many seasoned industrial security representatives, I feel like I know it all. I have been in this industry almost 25 years; I know where to look for answers, and I have my contacts. But one day it occurred to me just how much has changed during my career - enter the Internet, enter computer based training, enter instant security clearances (Interims), enter the JPAS/e-QIP interface, enter diminished contact with my cleared employees and visitors. Admitting that the contact with my cleared employees is not as intimate as it used to have to be, somehow I felt that I was losing touch with my own skill set because of it. You should consider buying the ISP Certification - The Industrial Security Professional Exam Manual, and spend 30 minutes with it each evening after work. Reinvigorate yourself. Give your imagination and professional growth some quiet stimulation. Remember. Refresh yourself. The best security education dollar you can spend, and not even leave home." Lisa Doman, Sierra Vista, AZ

"Jeff provides a paramount service with his book that assists in taking the ISP test. He gives insight into what is needed to help you be certified in the security industry today. Jeff's dedication and attention to detail is second to none and I highly recommend him on a professional level." Kenneth Wontz, President. Trinity Security Consultants, VA

*DOD Security Clearances and Contracts Guidebook*
"Jeffrey Bennett's comprehensive guide gives defense contractors all the information they need to establish and maintain a successful security program. He pulls together information from Presidential Executive Orders and regulations from numerous government agencies. Readers will learn how to appoint and train a facility security officer, navigate the security clearance process, win contracts dealing with classified information, and how to secure and protect that information."

"An excellent book for companies trying to get into the world of classified government contracts. It is a great starting point for new Facility Security Officers, telling them what they need to know in order to be successful at their job."

*How to Get U.S. Government Contracts and Classified Work*
"Loaded with insightful information about all of the concerns and roadblocks most small businesses have to get into the Defense industry. A must-have for new defense businesses and seasoned companies looking to improve their operations and security procedures."

"This book was extremely helpful and provides detailed information on how to get government contracts and classified work. It is a must for anyone wanting to get into government contracting. Jeff Bennett is knowledgeable on the topic and an expert. I highly recommend his book."

"With Jeff's bevy of knowledge and insight into DOD you are guaranteed to grow your book of business with the government. A must read for people who want to understand this landscape."

## Insider's Guide to Security Clearances

"Having been tasked with the mission to research all that I could about Security Clearances and the Facility Security Officer (FSO) position at a government contracting firm, it was difficult to find resources on the topic that were available for the up-and-coming FSO. In this book, Mr. Bennett gives clear and concise answers to help guide the way for those that haven't been in the industry for long or at all. And with the Kindle edition, it was easy to have the book with me for reference whenever I needed help with knowing which forms to use, what acronyms stand for, and what is the next step in the Security Clearance process."

"The book is great-- cuts to the point on how to get started in this business. Succinctly describes what you need to do to get your business set up to work on clearance contracts. Gives you helpful links, and does a fairly good job at listing out the "to-do's".

"Excellent for Defense professionals who want to understand and simplify the typically confusing landscape of security clearances. Jeff really knows his stuff and makes it very digestible to keep yourself safe and compliant!"

## *A special word of thanks and a favor to ask*

Thank you for buying my book. I really appreciate you being a reader and hope you find it helpful. If you have any questions, please feel free to contact me.

I would really love to hear your feedback and your input would help to make the next version of this book and my future books better. Please leave a helpful review, where you purchased your book, of what you thought of it.

I would also ask that you let a friend know about the book as well. Thanks so much and best of success to you!!

Jeffrey W. Bennett

Sign up for our reader newsletter:
*https://www.redbikepublishing.com/contact*

For more information on cleared defense contracting, security clearances, and training, check out our video.
*https://www.redbikepublishing.com/security/*

We also have cleared contractor, security clearance and National Industrial Security Program Operating Manual (NISPOM) training at Bennett Institute that could compliment your certification studies.
*https://www.bennettinstitute.com*

SFPC Master Exam Prep

Learn Faster, Retain More, Pass the Exam

Jeffrey W. Bennett, ISOC, ISP®, SAPPC, SFPC

# SFPC Master Exam Prep

## Learn Faster, Retain More, Pass the Exam

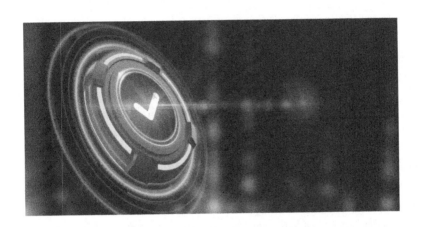

Jeffrey W. Bennett, ISOC, ISP®, SAPPC, SFPC

www.redbikepublishing.com

SFPC Master Exam Prep - Learn Faster, Retain More, Pass the Exam

Published by: Red Bike Publishing www.redbikepublishing.com Copyright © 2022 by Red Bike Publishing, LLC, Huntsville, Alabama

Published in the United States of America
www.redbikepublishing.com

Red Bike Publishing, LLC also publishes books in electronic format. Some publications appearing in print may not be available in electronic book format.
ISBN: 9781936800452
LCCN: 2022942222

# FROM THE AUTHOR

Congratulations on your decision to become SFPC certified. This is a big step and I'm so glad you made my book part of your journey. I believe that the study you undertake in these pages will be instrumental in your learning and in building confidence to take the exam. I recommend that you begin taking the first quiz immediately to determine how much you already know. Then I recommend studying the DoDM 5200 V. 1-3 books available online and also available in print at www.redbikepublishing.com. I have so many more recommendations later in this book, so keep reading.

During the past few years, I've been writing primarily about the certification opportunities with the National Industrial Security Program Operating Manual (NISPOM). It was my area of experience, and many security professionals were exploring the space and earning their certifications. These NISPOM based certifications included the Industrial Security Professional (ISP) and the Industrial Security Oversight Certification (ISOC). Both certifications were a great fit for the security professionals focused on NISPOM activities.

I've assisted hundreds of certification candidates with books and training, mainly helping to build test taking confidence and reducing stress by providing realistic testing scenarios. For many, I helped resolve a common issue of testers running out of time before they ran out of test. The practice exams helped many complete the test sooner and with more accurate answers than those who were less prepared.

During this time, the Department of Defense also implemented other certification opportunities. I began to receive requests for Security Fundamentals Professional Certification (SFPC) test preparation and thus began developing this study guide. My wish for you is the best of success as you use this guide to augment your studies. Be sure to dive right in with the practice questions. You will probably get a lot of answers wrong at first, but that should be expected; keep going. Review these questions time and again. Switch the order of the questions again and again until you become very familiar with the material. Set a clock and go through the questions, giving yourself no more than 2 minutes per question. Then reduce that time. Train the way you will test, so that when test day comes, you will be prepared.

In this book, you will see that I attempt to demonstrate the importance of not only becoming certified but leveraging the prep time as well as the final certification to become more effective at your important task of developing security programs to protect classified information. You are already beginning the important process as you build networks, obtain professional and academic education, and find mentors. Credibility is the key to influence and learning from others in the industry helps you build confidence in your decisions and capabilities. I also provide ideas to those of you might be stove piped in your career to expand your experience with more tasks as outlined in DoD 5200.01 V1-3. Helpful hints increase experience, confidence and provide ideas for hands on training. You can also join our newsletter for updates, security awareness ideas, and NISP topics. Register for my education rich newsletter at https://www.redbikepublishing.com/contact.

## DEDICATION

This book is dedicated to the men and women of all vocations and walks of life who defend our country and protect our nation's secrets.

## ACKNOWLEDGEMENT

None of this would have been possible without the loving support of my family. You have so willingly provided encouragement while understanding my need to write this book.

I would also like to thank Shama Patel for her social media support and editing services. You can reach her at Evening Light Designs, LLC at https://www.eveninglightdesigns.com.

# Disclaimer

This book is designed to give practice questions to those who are eligible to take the certifications such as the SFPC and other Security Professional Education Development (SPēD) certifications. I have written this book with the understanding that it will assist with exam studies, but should not be used as a standalone product. Our intention is to compliment career experience and DoD guidance.

All security and compliance related issues that you may face should be pursued with your government agency or Cognizant Security Office. This book is also designed to help the reader draw from experience and suggests ways to study for and take certification exams. Those who are new to the field can use this as a career guide to assist with gathering institutional knowledge until able to take the certification exam. However, in all cases this is not a guaranteed single source option for passing the exam. My intent is to present practice questions to prepare you for the test experience and not to suggest actual questions that may be found in any certification exam. I do not know what those actual questions may be.

As an ISP® and SPēD certified author, I have made every effort to make this manual as accurate and complete as possible. Some of the most experienced security specialists in the business have reviewed and edited this product.

# Table of Contents

From the Author                                          13

Dedication                                               15

Acknowledgement                                          15

Disclaimer                                               16

**CHAPTER 1 WHY YOU SHOULD GET A CERTIFICATION**         **19**

Getting Started                                          20

Developing a Plan                                        20

Seek additional study resources.                         21

Find a mentor.                                           22

Education                                                22

Experience                                               23

Study Groups                                             24

Additional Resources                                     25

**CHAPTER 2 DODM 5200.01**                               **27**

**PRACTICE TESTS**                                       **31**

TEST 1                                                   33

TEST 2                                                   55

TEST 3                                                   77

TEST 4                                                   99

**PRACTICE TEST ANSWERS**                                **119**

TEST 1 answers-Long Version                              121

TEST 2 answers-Long Version                              145

TEST 3 answers-Long Version                              169

TEST 4 - Long Answer                                     193

Test 1 Short Version                                     215

Test 2 Short Version                                     216

Test 3 Short Version                                     217

Test 4 Short Version                                     218

**WHAT NEXT?**                                           **219**

# CHAPTER 1 WHY YOU SHOULD GET A CERTIFICATION

Thanks again for buying this book. I am so glad you did and wish you well in your journey to become a SPeD certified professional. Security professionals who either desire certification or oversee careers of those who do, don't always know where to go to find information on what might be expected of them. Some might form study groups, take online training, find a mentor, but still lack actual practice questions focused on DoD guidance.

I began writing my first book while preparing for the ISP® Certification exam. I would study sections of NISPOM, rehearsing chapter and subchapter topics, writing practice questions, performing self-inspections, and interviewing ISP®s. Since most people I spoke with stated the biggest obstacle was running out of time, I wanted to answer the question: "How do I complete a 110 question open book test about the NISPOM during a 120 minute session?"

I realized that memorization would not be a good method for this test. More likely, I needed to consider the NISPOM structure and how to apply it. The NISPOM is an administrative guidance document describing what should be done to protect classified information, but not how to do it. I expected that if I studied where to find answers and how to apply the NISPOM topically, I could complete the test in enough time to check my work.

That's exactly what happened. Using information I used to write the book, I completed the test in 90 minutes; 30 minutes to spare. I realized that my study method had proven successful and that I could teach it to others.

After becoming a seasoned SPeD certified professional, I used the same process to write this study guide. While there is sufficient content available at CDSE, there is not a compatible way to rehearse a test environment (a lot of questions in a short amount of time). While the CDSE provides courses, this book provides questions. This book is intended to augment that study material and provide proven study methodology to help you better understand the DoD guidance and how to apply it. You will have more confidence in your ability to answer all test questions in the amount of time provided. The following chapters will help you understand the NISPOM and give you access to four full length practice tests and many essay questions. So, let's get started.

## GETTING STARTED

Developing a written plan is critical, helps maintain focus and keeps test anxiety at bay. It's easy to say, "next year I'll take the test." The tough part is maintaining the focus and discipline to get there. My recommended first step is to register and become approved to take the exam, select a date, and backward plan. Without the commitment triggered by registration, you may not have proper motivation to study in a timely manner.

### Developing a Plan

To reiterate, the first step is to register for the exam. This registration process ensures that you meet qualifications and are eligible to take the exam. Additionally, registering for the exam commits you to the event. If you wait until you are ready to take the exam, you may never feel "ready". The added pressure of an actual date can prove motivating. In most cases, you can register and schedule a test date up to one year in advance.

Next, get copies of DoDM 5200.01 V 1-3. For printed versions, please visit www.redbikepublishing.com for the manuals and related books and training. Read the manuals and become familiar with the material. Don't try to cram the entire series all at once as you risk losing that knowledge within minutes. Remember, we are going for a lifestyle and professional shake up. What we do in preparation for certification must stick with us throughout our careers. The purpose of this guide is not only to help you pass the test, but to become proficient, implement effective programs and increase your ability to protect our nation's assets.

It is not necessary to memorize the manuals, just become familiar with where to find the information in the performance of your duties. You need to not only be able to access information for your job, but you need to answer the questions in an allotted amount of time. Become familiar with the content to answer the following questions:

What do chapters cover?
What categories do paragraphs and sections explain?
How do the manual sections apply to your craft?

Make it part of your daily regimen to relate the chapter to the subject.

Seek additional study resources.

You should primarily start with the organizations who oversee or facilitate the certification. For the SFPC it's CDSE. I highly recommend focusing study time there and use this book to test your knowledge. Visit their websites and become familiar with their training available @ https://www.cdse.edu. Go to the website to find all the information necessary to qualify and register for the SFPC certification exam. Additionally, there are links to DoD recommended training.

I also recommend books about the NISP such as my book How to Get U.S. Government Contracts and Classified Work which is a chapter by chapter walk through of the NISPOM and how to apply it. It's not necessarily about the DoDMs covering SFPC, but the protection concepts are similar. Additionally, each chapter has review questions that you can answer on how to apply the security lessons. Next, use this book to supplement that training with practice tests.

Find a mentor.

Humans are meant to be part of a team. We work best when we work together. Loads are carried farther, work levels are reduced significantly, and costs have less impact. You may already work within a large security team. However, I recommend that you find a mentor who will challenge you to step outside of your organization and comfort zone.

A mentor can share experiences with you. They will have demonstrated expertise in their fields, have a good reputation within the industry and will know how to direct you to find answers to your concerns. Your mentor should be a cheerleader who knows your goals and would appreciate seeing you reach success. They will call on you to check progress or meet with you for questions. This relationship will reach beyond the certification goal as mentors coach you through life. This person does not badmouth others or talk you out of your goals; nobody has time for that.

For additional support, consider joining or starting a study group. It's good to be accountable to both a mentor and a peer group. You may find that there are many local security specialists who would love to join you in your goals. If no one is local, consider using available resources to start web conferences or other online study platforms.

Education

This study guide can assist you with the electronic version of the test. Also, be sure to obtain hard copy or electronic versions of the SF86, DD Form 254, SF 312, database user manuals, and other resources helpful to your profession. You may find many questions from the exam addressed to those resources.

## Experience

Another stone on your path is to work on different security projects. You can do this internal or external to your organization. For example, if you are working in personnel security and your primary function is to request security clearances, volunteer to learn about other security functions like classified contract management.

Subcontracting, performance of classified work, facility and personnel clearance directives are driven by the DD Form 254. Stepping into this new world will give insight into personnel security functions and offer a broader perspective of security duties necessary. This is beneficial for further career development and familiarization with SFPC exam topics.

Consider volunteering to conduct some of the tasks found in organization oversight such as security audits or inspections. This will give you an opportunity to study requirements, evaluate progress, make decisions, correct problems, and advise in all areas of security. If you want to separate yourself from the mediocre performers, step out and assume the role. You will amaze yourself with the exponentially increasing skills developed from interaction with different security areas while serving as an assessment or self-review leader.

If you are really feeling adventurous, put together a self-review team. As the leader, you can meet regularly with your team to discuss findings, develop corrective courses of action, brief results, and recommend solutions. In this leadership capacity, you will accelerate your learning curve. Other professionals will soon approach you for solutions, thus improving your self-confidence.

This is also a great time to dive into the world of physical security. You can interact with security guards and work with them as they conduct their routes and questions concerning physical security requirements. Volunteer to be on call. There is nothing like being the "go-to" person at 2:00 am while responding to alarms. Such situations require study of policies and NISPOM requirements and ability to react to stressful events.

If your mission makes it possible, step into new opportunities with certifying closed areas and vaults. It is one thing to read about requirements and quite another to personally go through the checklists. This will prepare you for questions concerning false ceilings, construction requirements, and intrusion detection systems. The point is to get involved with all aspects of security and away from your comfort zone. Besides becoming certification worthy, you may find yourself rewarded in other ways.

Study Groups

There are many ways to form a study group. As mentioned earlier, humans are made for companionship and teamwork. Study groups facilitate learning as everyone shares experiences and helps each other find answers. You will also be able to hold each other accountable, write practice tests, and encourage one another. Concentrate on studying for the exam and make it the primary focus. Write a study plan, keep an agenda and assign someone in the group responsible for enforcing the rules and keeping focus.

In keeping with the theme of certification being part of career development, study groups offer other benefits such as instant networking. There, you may find an audience of security professionals with a wide range of expertise and have many experiences that they would love to share. The benefit of being in a network is greater than the amount of the members. At some point in your career (more often than not) you may find that you may have questions or concerns about organizational security policies and how they support the national objectives. Would it not be nice to have someone to bring those concerns to who will give sound advice with no penalties? Also, guess where you might be able to find one of your mentors?

As you continue to improve your skills, take a moment to visualize what certification will bring to your career. Ask yourself how it will

distinguish you from your peers. You may be inspired to uphold
the ethical standards of the certification. You may be motivated by
having to work to continuously learn, publish, teach, and encourage
keeping your certification current. Perhaps you will be inspired by
the prestige and credibility the certification brings to you and your
profession. Perhaps you want the title to put in your business card, or
the certificate for your wall. Whatever the motivation, use it to propel
yourself toward the goal of earning your next certification.

## Additional Resources

Be sure to check out the last few pages of this book for additional
resources to assist you with your studies and other certifications.

# CHAPTER 2 DODM 5200.01

One last thing before we get started on practice questions. I recommend spending some time getting to know DoDM 5200.01 Volumes 1-3, which we will now refer to as "Manual". Don't rely on your ability to answer these questions as they may or may not be on the test. You can measure successful study as your ability to answer these practice questions because of your familiarity with the source material. It's important to understand how to apply the material covered in the volumes, not memorize the information.

Spend your time studying each volume by title and then the material in each volume topically. This will provide a better understanding of how to answer questions and how to apply what you will have learned. For example, if the question asks about classification and Original Classification Authority, you would understand that the answer can be found in Volume 2.

This means that having studied Manual Volume 2, you will understand topically how the OCA uses a step-based process to apply classification. From there, you should be able to confidently answer any other classification or classification marking questions.

Additionally, you will be able to use this information to reasonably deduct the correct answer. So, instead of just charging through the questions, dedicate time to study the volumes topically and use the sample test questions to reinforce your knowledge.

The DoD provides restrictions, rules, guidelines, and procedures for preventing unauthorized disclosure of classified material; it is the primary regulatory reference for performing industrial security. The Manual applies to authorized users of classified information and equips those providing security services with the critical instruction on how to implement the Manual in their organizations. It is up to the user to provide accurate interpretation of the guidelines to the specific requirements.

The user should apply the concept of Risk Management while implementing the Manual. There are three factors necessary in determining risk. The first is the level of damage to national security that could be reasonably expected to result from unauthorized disclosure of classified material. It is important to know that the Manual provides guidance on how to identify and protect classified items at all levels.

Though the Manual provides guidance, it doesn't tell you how to execute. It is up to the user to determine how to apply it for test purposes. In real life, the security specialist interprets the Manual and applies it to their organization.

The Manual is the security specialist's go-to source for conducting the business of protecting our nation's resources. Becoming familiar with the Manual's contents will assist the with establishing a security program, assist oversight organizations with what to inspect, and assists certification exam subjects with where to find answers and helps formulate the answers. Far greater in context, the Manual is to be used as a guide that can only help improve national security with a good and positive working model.

The designated security specialist develops the skills to run the organization's security program. This means knowing how to interpret the Manual and explain it to the organization. The security specialist should learn the organization subject matter expert's language and let them know how they contribute to the organization's success. The security specialist's job is to have the Manual make sense, and as the SFPC certification exam participant, you should also learn it well.

I understand taking such a certification endeavor is scary. Most will not certify only because they fear failure or fear test taking in general. Don't let that stop you. Register for the test and take it as many times as you can until you pass it. Don't let fear stand in the way.

However, there are a few things you can do to soar past the fear and succeed at testing. That success depends on taking practice tests. Set up your practice tests to simulate the stress of test day. I want to recommend a few study methods that I had tremendous success with.

Read the Manual and paraphrase the contents. Begin with paraphrasing the entire Manual into a few sentences. Then paraphrase each volume independently. This will help you understand what each section covers.

In the earlier example, you might look at Volume 2 and paraphrase the role each player has in its application.

Also, enroll in CDSE and take all the courses you can. Even if you know all the material. Even if you don't have time, make the time to take all the course exams. Here's a helpful hint, download the PDF version of the course transcripts prior to taking the course exam. Then start the exam and practice searching for the answers. Even if you know the answers, search until you can find them.

Go through each question in this book and use the Manual to search for answers. Again, even if you know the answer, do the search. This will give you practice and help increase your test taking confidence. Go through this book as many times as you can until you are confident that you can find the answers. Believe me, it will be a skill you will always need.

Set a timer. Use the questions in this book. For each test, set the timer for 120 minutes. Then set it for 90 minutes. Then try 60. The added pressure of a time limit and even a condensed time line will make you more resilient on test day.

Are you ready? Then turn the page and begin practicing. Good luck!

# PRACTICE TESTS

1. Use paperback copy available at www.redbikepublishing. com or download online version of DODM 5200.01 V 1-3 to search for answers.

2. Select the best answer for each choice.

3. Once complete, check your answers against the answer keys in the back of this book.

**Warning: Not all questions will have searchable answers. It is important to understand the spirit of the question and know which part of the manual contains the answer.**

# TEST 1

1.   Which statement best reflects the purpose of the DoD Information Security Program?
   a.   Provides overarching program guidance and direction for the DoD Information Security Program
   b.   Provides ideas for DoD Information Security Program Implementation
   c.   Provides raining and resources for DoD Information Security Program
   d.   Provides executive direction for all DoD security disciplines
   e.   None of the above

2.   Which of the following are potential sanctions for violating provisions of DoDM 5200.01?
   a.   A warning
   b.   Forfeiture of pay
   c.   Discharge
   d.   A. and b.
   e.   All of the above

3.   Which of the following is not a policy for the retention of classified information?
   a.   Shall be maintained only when it is required for effective and efficient operation of the organization
   b.   Shall be maintained only when it is required if law requires its retention
   c.   Shall be maintained if treaty requires its retention
   d.   Shall be maintained if international agreement requires its retention
   e.   All apply

4. How does the term "need-to-know," relate to protecting classified information?

a. All program managers have need to know of all aspects of their project

b. Determined primarily by rank and position

c. An official determination for access to specific classified information for a lawful and authorized governmental function

d. An official determination for blanket access to all classified information for a lawful and authorized governmental function

e. Need to know is an expectation for all government civilians

5. How does the term "access," relate to protecting classified information?

a. The right to access classified information

b. The ability to access classified information

c. The acceptance of classified information

d. The opportunity to access classified information

e. B. and d.

6. Which is not an access requirement for protecting Confidential information?

a. Non-disclosure agreement

b. Confidential security clearance

c. Need to know

d. Badge card

e. All are access requirements

7. Which is not an access requirement for protecting Secret information?

a. Non-disclosure agreement

b. Confidential security clearance Badge card

c. Need to know

d. Secret security clearance

e. All are access requirements

8. Which is not an access requirement for protecting Top Secret information?
   a. Non-disclosure agreement
   b. Top Secret security clearance
   c. Need to know
   d. Secret security clearance
   e. All are access requirements

9. Which is a specific requirement for access to Sensitive Compartmented Information (SCI)?
   a. DNI authorized SCI-Non-disclosure agreement
   b. Top Secret security clearance
   c. Need to know
   d. Secret security clearance
   e. All are access requirements

10. Which is a specific requirement for access to Special Access Programs (SAP)?
    a. SCI-Non-disclosure agreement
    b. Top Secret security clearance
    c. Need to know
    d. Secret security clearance
    e. DoD approved program indoctrination

11. Which is a specific requirement for access to NATO information?
    a. SCI-Non-disclosure agreement
    b. Top Secret security clearance
    c. Need to know
    d. Secret security clearance
    e. Written acknowledgment of NATO briefing

12. What is original classification?
    a.   A first edition classified document from which all subsequent documents are numbered
    b.   An initial determination that information needs protection against unauthorized disclosure
    c.   A derived decision that information needs protection against unauthorized disclosure
    d.   The very first classified document created post WWII
    e.   None of the above

13. Who has the authority to originally classify information?
    a.   Prime contractor
    b.   Government employees regardless of position
    c.   Individual authorized in writing to do so
    d.   A. and c.
    e.   All of the above

14. Which is not a step of the original classification process?
    a.   Determine if information is owned by the U.S. Government
    b.   Determine if information has not already been classified
    c.   Determine level of national embarrassment disclosure would create
    d.   Determine and assign the appropriate level of classification
    e.   Determine the appropriate duration of classification

15. Which is a role of the Original Classification Authority (OCA) in changing classification level?
    a.   Any appointed OCA can change classification level regardless of jurisdiction
    b.   An OCA can change the classification level of a document, but not the portion markings
    c.   An OCA can update security classification guides
    d.   An OCA is not permitted to communicate classification level changes
    e.   An OCA cannot authorize the re-marking of classification level changes

16. Which information is not found within a Security Classification Guide?
   a. Specific items of information to be protected
   b. Specific classification of information
   c. Specific reason for classification
   d. State declassification instructions
   e. Determine level of national embarrassment disclosure would create

17. Which information is not found within a Security Classification Guide?
   a. Specific items of information to be protected
   b. Specific classification of information
   c. Specific reason for classification
   d. State declassification instructions
   e. Estimated cost of protecting classified information

18. What is tentative classification?
   a. Final classification
   b. Derived classified information
   c. Classification duration
   d. Classification pending approval of an OCA
   e. Classified items awaiting input into a Security Classification Guide

19. Which is not a classification duration option?
   a. A date or independently verifiable event less than 10 years from the date of original classification
   b. A date 10 years from the date of original classification
   c. A date 25 years from the date of original classification
   d. A date 55 years from the date of original classification
   e. A date or independently verifiable event greater than 10 and less than 25 years from the date of original classification

20. Which is a classification duration option for originally classified information?
   a.   A date or independently verifiable event less than 10 years from the date of original classification
   b.   A date 10 years from the date of original classification
   c.   A date 25 years from the date of original classification
   d.   A date or independently verifiable event greater than 10 and less than 25 years from the date of original classification
   e.   All of the above

21. Which cover sheet is appropriate for Secret information?
   a.   SF 701
   b.   SF 702
   c.   SF 703
   d.   SF 704
   e.   SF 705

22. Which is a classification duration option for originally classified information?
   a.   A date or independently verifiable event less than 10 years from the date of original classification
   b.   A date 7 years from the date of original classification
   c.   A date 20 years from the date of original classification
   d.   A date or independently verifiable event greater than 5 and less than 15 years from the date of original classification
   e.   "50X1-HUM," designating a duration of up to 75 years from the date of original classification

23. The purpose of declassification instructions is to identify:
   a.   A date or independently verifiable event less than 10 years from the date of original classification
   b.   A date 7 years from the date of original classification
   c.   A date 20 years from the date of original classification
   d.   A date or independently verifiable event greater than 5 and less than 15 years from the date of original classification
   e.   "50X1-HUM," designating a duration of up to 75 years from the

date of original classification

24. What are the requirements for protecting information under the Patent Secrecy Act of 1952?
   a. The Department of Defense shall handle a patent application on which a secrecy order has been imposed
   b. All patents from the U.S. Government and contractors should be classified
   c. Patents cannot contain classified information
   d. Department of Justice handles all patents and the protection of patents
   e. Inventions are in the public domain, therefore cannot be classified

25. Which of the following is a consideration for developing a tetragraph?
   a. Must be three alphabetic characters
   b. Must be four alphabetic characters
   c. Must be five alphabetic characters
   d. Must be four alphanumeric characters
   e. Associated membership list must change frequently

26. What are the requirements for protecting Nuclear Command and Control-Extremely Sensitive Information (NC2-ESI)?
   a. NC2-ESI information shall be marked, safeguarded, and distributed in accordance with 32CFR Part 117
   b. NC2-ESI information shall be marked, safeguarded, and distributed in accordance with DoDM 5200.01 Vol 2
   c. NC2-ESI information shall be marked, safeguarded, and distributed in accordance with CJCS Instruction 3231.01B
   d. NC2-ESI information shall be marked, safeguarded, and distributed in accordance with DoDM 5200.01 Vol 1
   e. NC2-ESI information shall be marked, safeguarded, and distributed in accordance with DoDM 5200.01 Vol 3

27. Which principles are used when challenging a classification decision?
   a.  The holder should communicate issue with a security manager or the OCA to bring about any necessary correction
   b.  The holder may informally question classification
   c.  The holder should provide a sufficient description of information being challenged
   d.  A. and c.
   e.  All of the above

28. Which of the following is a correct procedure to use when challenging a classification decision?
   a.  Forward challenges through appropriate channels
   b.  Provide a general description of information being challenged
   c.  Holders should seek approval through their immediate supervisor prior to challenging information
   d.  Justification is rarely required
   e.  All of the above

29. Which principles and procedures are used when extending classification duration?
   a.  OCA immediately notifies all known holders of information
   b.  OCA notifies the GCA of all changes
   c.  OCA notifies FSOs of changes
   d.  No action necessary if within 25 years from date of document's origin
   e.  Information becomes declassified if no action is taken

30. What is derivative classification?
   a.  Information classified by an OCA
   b.  Information copied from an originally classified document
   c.  Information paraphrased from an originally classified document
   d.  Information duplicated from an originally classified document
   e.  Information classified by a contractor

31. Which of the following is not a step in the derivative classification process?
   a. Determine if information contains classified information
   b. Derived information should be portion marked
   c. Determine the duration of classification
   d. Contact the originator of classified document or consult the explanation
   e. All are steps

32. Which authorized sources of security classification guidance can be used in the derivative classification process?
   a. The senior security officer
   b. Open source research
   c. Contradicting sources
   d. All of the above
   e. None of the above

33. Which is not among the responsibilities of derivative classifiers in protecting classified information?
   a. Observe and respect the OCA classification determination
   b. Do not identify themselves as a derivative classifier
   c. Use only authorized sources
   d. Use caution when restating information
   e. Take appropriate steps to resolve doubt

34. Which classification considerations are associated with the concept of compilation?
   a. Does not reflect any OCA considerations
   b. Elements do not need to be located where one could consider an association
   c. The final decision of classification of compiled data resides with the holder
   d. Classification by compilation requires an OCA decision
   e. The fact that a lot of information is collocated means that it is classified

35. Classification involving the DoD acquisition process shall conform to which of the following?
   a.   DoDD 5000.01
   b.   DoDD 5200.44
   c.   DoDI 5000.02
   d.   A. and c.
   e.   All of the above

36. Which classification considerations are associated with information released to the public?
   a.   Information declassified without proper authority remains classified
   b.   Information that has been released after declassification can be reclassified under certain circumstances
   c.   Classified information that has been released without proper authority remains classified
   d.   A. and b.
   e.   All of the above

37. Which classification considerations are associated with information released through the Freedom of Information Act (FOIA)?
   a.   There are none as FOIA overrides classification
   b.   Classified information is exempt from FOIA processes
   c.   The OCA should provide a description of damage with consideration to any FOIA request
   d.   A. and c.
   e.   A. and b.

38. Which classification considerations are associated with non-government research and development information?
   a.   Products are not eligible for classification
   b.   The government must acquire a proprietary interest first
   c.   The government has an obligation to classified anything under R&D
   d.   The non-government entity developing R&D effort requests control under the classification system

e.   B. and d.

39. Which classification considerations are associated the Patent Secrecy Act of 1952?
   a.   Secretary of Defense may determine that a patent disclosure could cause damage to national security
   b.   When the patent contains classified information it shall be protected according to classification level
   c.   If patent contains CUI it must be protected accordingly
   d.   All of the above
   e.   B. and d.

40. Which is identified to be responsible for the overall management, functioning, and effectiveness of the information security program within their respective DoD Component?
   a.   WHS
   b.   Heads of DoD Components
   c.   DoD CIO
   d.   Undersecretary of Defense
   e.   USD

41. Which of the following are identified as authorities for declassification?
   a.   Cognizant OCA
   b.   Those who have been delegated declassification authority
   c.   NSA/CSS
   d.   A. and b.
   e.   All of the above

42. Which information is found within a Security Declassification Guide?

a. Information for an effective review of classified information

b. Information for an effective declassification of classified information

c. Information for a reclassification of declassified information

d. A. and b.

e. All of the above

43. Which are the requirements for protecting Restricted Data (RD)?

a. RD can be emailed to anyone with the appropriate clearance and need to know

b. RD can be emailed to only those who have received additional briefings

c. RD information must be password protected

d. Systems containing RD do not need certification

e. A. and c.

44. Which policies protect SCI?

a. Applicable national policy

b. Policies established by DNI and implement DoD issuance

c. DoDM 5200.01-V1

d. A. and c.

e. All of the above

45. Which policies protect SAP information?

a. Reference (q)

b. Reference (at)

c. DoDM 5200.01-V1

d. B. and c.

e. All of the above

46. Which policies protect foreign government information (FGI)?
a. Reference (d)
b. Reference (u)
c. DoDM 5200.01-V3
d. International agreements
e. All of the above

47. What are the processes associated with downgrading or upgrading classified information?
a. Line through old markings
b. Erase old markings
c. Destroy declassified items and reproduce new declassified ones
d. Remove cover pages
e. All of the above

48. Which are not authorized security classifications?
a. Portion marking indicating C, S, TS
b. Restricted, Secret, Top Secret
c. Confidential, Secret, Top Secret
d. Unclassified, Registered, Secret
e. In Confidence, Secret, Restricted

49. Which elements are required on classified information?
a. Overall classification
b. Office of origin
c. Upgrading instructions
d. Only page and portion markings are required
e. A. and b.

50. Which of the following are authorized dissemination markings?
a. FOR OFFICIAL USE ONLY
b. FOR SHOW
c. FOR DISPLAY
d. CONTROLLED INFORMATION
e. NOT AUTHORIZED FOR RELEASE

51. Which are control markings?
a. Used in banners
b. Separated by classification level with //
c. May be used multiple times on the same line
d. Identify special control systems
e. All of the above

52. What are trigraphs?
a. Used to identify countries
b. Used to identify international organizations
c. Used to identify international alliances
d. A. and c.
e. All of the above

53. What are tetragraphs?
a. Used to identify country names
b. Used to identify international organizations
c. Used to identify international alliances
d. b and c
e. All of the above

54. Which statement best describes "unauthorized disclosure?"
a. Transfer of classified information outside of the United States
b. Transfer of classified information outside of an organization
c. Transfer of controlled unclassified information to an unauthorized recipient
d. Transfer of controlled unclassified information outside of a facility
e. None of the above

55. Which are methods for destruction of non-IT media?
a. Degaussing
b. Sanding
c. Chemical decomposition
d. Mutilation
e. All of the above

56. Which statement best describes a security infraction?
a. Failure to comply with security requirements
b. Security incident resulting in compromise of classified information
c. Security incident that does not constitute a violation
d. A. and c.
e. None of the above

57. Which statement best describes a security violation?
a. Failure to comply with security requirements
b. Security incident resulting in compromise of classified information
c. Security incident that does not constitute a violation
d. A.and c.
e. None of the above

58. Which statement best describes a compromise?
a. Failure to comply with security requirements
b. Unauthorized disclosure to an unauthorized person
c. Classified information that cannot be located
d. A. and c.
e. None of the above

59. Which statement best describes a loss?
a. Failure to comply with security requirements
b. Unauthorized disclosure to an unauthorized person
c. Security incident that does not constitute a violation
d. Classified information that cannot be located
e. All of the above

60. Which are the requirements for reporting a security infraction?
   a.   It requires a full investigation at any occurrence
   b.   It requires an inquiry at all occurrences
   c.   Infractions can lead to full investigations
   d.   A. and c.
   e.   None of the above

61. Which are the requirements for reporting a security violation?
   a.   It requires a full investigation at any occurrence
   b.   It requires an inquiry at all occurrences
   c.   Infractions can lead to full investigations
   d.   A. and c.
   e.   None of the above

62. Which are the characteristics of an inquiry?
   a.   Fact finding analysis
   b.   Conducted to determine if there is a loss of classified information
   c.   Conducted to determine if classified information was disclosed in an unauthorized manner
   d.   A. and c.
   e.   All of the above

63. Which are the characteristics of an investigation?
   a.   Conducted when incident cannot be resolved through inquiry
   b.   Conducted to determine if there is a loss of classified information
   c.   Conducted to determine if classified information was disclosed in an unauthorized manner
   d.   Conducted when a security violation where in-depth examination is required
   e.   All of the above

64. Control measures for safeguarding classified information against unauthorized access may include which of the following?
a. Personnel
b. Physical
c. Technical
d. A. and c.
e. All of the above

65. When are administrative controls required?
a. When personnel controls are insufficient
b. When physical controls are insufficient
c. When technical controls are insufficient
d. A. and c.
e. All of the above

66. Which of the following are examples of administrative controls?
a. Records of internal distribution of classified information
b. Records of access to classified information
c. Records of generation of classified information
d. Records of inventory of classified information
e. All of the above

67. Which of the following are some custodial responsibilities of individuals to safeguard classified materials?
a. Control access to classified information
b. Practice proper measures for storing classified information
c. Conduct security clearance investigation
d. A. and c.
e. A. and b.

68. Which of the following should be provided during initial orientation?
    a. Definition of classified information
    b. How to conduct security incident investigations
    c. A basic understanding of security policies
    d. A. and b.
    e. A. and c.


69. Which manual addresses security incidents involving Alternative Compensatory Control Measures (ACCM)?
    a. DoDM 5200.01 Vol 3, Enclosure 2
    b. DODM 5200.01 Vol 2, Enclosure 2
    c. 32 CFR Part 117, Paragraph 20
    d. DoDI 5220.01, Enclosure 3
    e. DoDM 5400.02


70. Concerning employees outside the executive branch, which of the following statements is false?
    a. Must be necessary for a lawful use
    b. Does not need to be permitted by OCA
    c. Must be necessary for authorized used
    d. Recipient eligibility should be determined
    e. None of the above


71. Which are requirements for protecting open storage classified materials at the SECRET level?
    a. A senior official determines that security in depth is provided
    b. A cleared employee will inspect area during four hour periods
    c. An IDS response team should arrive within 30 minutes of alarm
    d. All of the above
    e. None of the above

72. Which of the following statements are most accurate as described for the destruction of classified IT?
    a. Overwriting and degaussing
    b. Degaussing and sanding
    c. Sanding and overwriting
    d. Overwriting, sanding and physical destruction
    e. Sanding, degaussing, overwriting and physical destruction

73. Which are the authorized methods for the transmission / transportation of Confidential classified information?
    a. U.S. Postal Service standard mail
    b. U.S. Postal Service registered mail
    c. Commercial carrier, but no requirement for surveillance service
    d. On U.S. ships, but no receipt or agreement is necessary
    e. On any ship with any registry as long as receipts are provided

74. Which are the purposes and basic concepts involved in properly preparing Secret materials for transportation?
    a. Outer wrapper must have individuals name
    b. Outer wrapper must contain classification level
    c. A briefcase may serve as an outer wrapper
    d. Specialized shipping containers may not serve as outer wrapper
    e. All of the above

75. Which actions are authorized for hand carrying classified materials?
    a. The information is already available at the delivery address
    b. The lack of operational necessity exists
    c. There are secure communications available
    d. Arrangements have been made for security storage
    e. All of the above

76. Which are general requirements governing the transfer of classified information or material to Foreign Governments?
    a. Transfers could occur in the continental U.S.
    b. Transfers of classified information only occur outside of the continental U.S.
    c. Recipients must be designated by recipient government
    d. A. and c.
    e. B. and c.


77. Which are general requirements governing the transfer of classified information or material to Foreign Governments?
    a. Transfers shall be conducted through contractor to contractor channels
    b. Letters of Agreement require detailed transfer instructions
    c. Recipients must be designated by recipient government
    d. A. and b.
    e. B. and c.


78. Which are the attributes of confidentiality as it relates to information security?
    a. Ensure that data remains available
    b. Ensure that data remains trusted
    c. Ensure data remains unavailable to unauthorized persons
    d. Ensure users know who they are communicating with
    e. Loss of ability to authenticate


79. The Director of National Intelligence prescribes the sections of the Manual that address _____ and _____ including _____.
    a. Operations, intelligence sources, procurement
    b. Intelligence sources, methods, SCI
    c. SAP, intelligence sources, means
    d. Organization, classification, procurement
    e. Classification, dissemination, intelligence sources

80. Which are the attributes of integrity relating to information security?
    a.  Ensure that data remains available
    b.  Ensure that data remains trusted
    c.  Ensure data remains unavailable to unauthorized persons
    d.  Ensure users know who they are communicating with
    e.  Loss of ability to authenticate

81. Which are the attributes of availability relating to information security?
    a.  Ensure that data remains accessible
    b.  Ensure that data remains trusted
    c.  Ensure data remains unavailable to unauthorized persons
    d.  Ensure users know who they are communicating with
    e.  Loss of ability to authenticate

82. Which are the attributes of non-repudiation as relating to information security?
    a.  Ensure that data remains accessible
    b.  Ensure that data remains trusted
    c.  Ensure data remains unavailable to unauthorized persons
    d.  Ensure users know who they are communicating with
    e.  Loss of ability to authenticate

83. Which are methods for destruction of IT media?
    a.  Overwriting
    b.  Sanding
    c.  Chemical decomposition
    d.  A. and b.
    e.  All of the above

84. What is the impact of cybersecurity lapses on confidentiality?
   a.  Data may not be available
   b.  Data may not be trusted
   c.  Data may be available to unauthorized persons
   d.  Users may not be sure of whom they are communicating with
   e.  Loss of ability to authenticate

85.  What are some characteristics of system categorization?
   a.  Requires determination of impact of confidence, integration and availability
   b.  Requires determination of impact of confidence, integrity and availability
   c.  Requires determination of impact of confidential, secret and top secret
   d.  Requires determination of impact of confidentiality, integrity, and availability
   e.  Requires determination of impact of confidentiality, integrity, and availableness

86.  Which is true of a data spill?
   a.  The activity security manager has overall responsibility of network operations
   b.  The activity security manager ensures policy requirements are met
   c.  The IA staff ensures policy requirements are met
   d.  Users have overall responsibility of network operations
   e.  All of the above

# TEST 2

1.  Which best describes a purpose or scope of the DoD Information Security Program?
    a.  Provides executive direction for all DoD security disciplines with regard to declassification only
    b.  Provides overarching program guidance and direction for the DoD Information Security Program with regard to the classification, declassification, and protection of classified information
    c.  Provides ideas for DoD Information Security Program Implementation with regard to the classification, declassification, and protection of classified information
    d.  A. and b.
    e.  None of the above

2.  Which best explains the retention policy for classified and controlled unclassified information?
    a.  Shall be maintained only when it is required for effective and efficient operation of the organization
    b.  Shall be maintained if a law requires its retention
    c.  Shall be maintained if a treaty requires its retention
    d.  Shall be maintained if an international agreement requires its retention
    e.  All of the above

3.  Which document provides DoD policy concerning access to Formerly Restricted Data (FRD)?
    a.  DoDI 5210.02
    b.  DoDI 5200.44
    c.  DoDM 5200.01
    d.  DoDM 5300.02
    e.  None of the above

4. Which provides procedures and minimum security standards for the handling and protection of NATO classified information and was written by USD (P)?
    a. Reference (d)
    b. Reference (u)
    c. DoDM 5200.01-V3
    d. International agreements
    e. All of the above

5. Which is a specific requirement for access to NATO?
    a. SCI-Non-disclosure agreement
    b. Top Secret security clearance
    c. Need to know
    d. Secret security clearance
    e. Written acknowledgment of NATO briefing

6. Which is not a step of the original classification process?
    a. Determine if information is owned by the U.S. Government
    b. Determine if information has not already been classified
    c. Determine level of national embarrassment that disclosure would create
    d. Determine and assign the appropriate level of classification
    e. Determine the appropriate duration of classification

7. Which is a classification duration option for originally classified information?
    a. A date or independently verifiable event less than 10 years from the date of original classification
    b. A date 7 years from the date of original classification
    c. A date 20 years from the date of original classification
    d. A date or independently verifiable event greater than 5 and less than 15 years from the date of original classification
    e. "50X1-HUM," designating a duration of up to 75 years from the date of original classification

8. Which authorized sources of security classification guidance can be used in the derivative classification process?
   a. The OCA
   b. Originator of source document
   c. Security Classification Guides
   d. All of the above
   e. None of the above

9. Which classification considerations are associated the Patent Secrecy Act of 1952?
   a. Secretary of Defense may determine that a patent disclosure could cause damage to national security
   b. When the patent contains classified information it shall be protected according to classification level
   c. If patent contains CUI it must be protected accordingly
   d. All of the above
   e. B. and d.

10. Which of the following are identified as authorities for declassification?
    a. Cognizant OCA
    b. Those who have been delegated declassification authority
    c. NSA/CSS
    d. All of the above
    e. A. and b.

11. Which document provides DoD policy concerning access to Formerly Restricted Data (FRD)?
    a. DoDI 5210.02
    b. DoDI 5200.44
    c. DoDM 5200.01
    d. DoDM 5300.02
    e. None of the above

12. Which policies are referred to for protecting NATO and FGI information?
   a. Reference (d)
   b. Reference (u)
   c. DoDM 5200.01-V3
   d. International agreements
   e. All of the above

13. Which of the following are authorized dissemination markings?
   a. FOR SHOW
   b. CONTROLLABLE IMAGERY
   c. FOR DISPLAY
   d. CONTROLLED INFORMATION
   e. NOT AUTHORIZED FOR RELEASE

14. Which of the following is untrue concerning requirements for protecting open storage classified materials at the CONFIDENTIAL level?
   a. A senior official determines that security in depth is provided
   b. A cleared employee will inspect area during four hour periods
   c. An IDS response team should arrive within 30 minutes of alarm
   d. All of the above
   e. None of the above

15. Which is not an access requirement for Top Secret?
   a. Non-disclosure agreement
   b. Top Secret security clearance
   c. Need to know
   d. Secret security clearance
   e. All of the above

16. Which statement best describes a security violation?
   a. Failure to comply with security requirements
   b. Security incident resulting in compromise of classified

information

    c.   Security incident that does not constitute a violation

    d.   A. and c.

    e.   None of the above

17.  What are the requirements for reporting a security infraction?

    a.   It requires a full investigation at any occurrence

    b.   It requires an inquiry at all occurrences

    c.   Infractions can lead to full investigations

    d.   A. and c.

    e.   None of the above

18.  Which of the following are examples of administrative controls?

    a.   Records of internal distribution of classified information

    b.   Records of access to classified information

    c.   Records of generation of classified information

    d.   Records of inventory of classified information

    e.   All of the above

19.  What are the attributes of availability as it relates to information security?

    a.   Ensure that data remains accessible

    b.   Ensure that data remains trusted

    c.   Ensure data remains unavailable to unauthorized persons

    d.   Ensure users know who they are communicating with

    e.   Loss of ability to authenticate

20.  Which are the authorized methods for the transmission/ transportation of Top Secret classified information?

    a.   From cleared person to cleared person as long as they have need to know

    b.   NSA approved electronic means

    c.   Defense Courier Service

    d.   DCS approved specialized shipping container

    e.   All of the above

21. Which of the following are true about need to know?
    a. All government employees have need to know
    b. All program managers have need to know of all aspects of their project
    c. Determined primarily by rank and position
    d. An official determination for access to all classified information for a lawful and authorized governmental function
    e. An official determination for access to specific classified information for a lawful and authorized governmental function

22. Which purpose and basic concepts are involved in properly preparing Confidential materials for transportation?
    a. Inner wrapper may contain individuals name
    b. Inner wrapper must not contain classification level
    c. A briefcase may serve as an outer wrapper
    d. For classified information that cannot be packaged and the outside is classified, no outer wrapper is necessary
    e. A. and c.

23. Which of the following provides the best definition of accessing classified information?
    a. The desire to access classified information
    b. The acceptance of classified information
    c. The opportunity to access classified information
    d. The right to access classified information
    e. All of the above

24. Which of the following is a consideration for hand carrying classified material?
    a. The availability at the delivery address
    b. Existence of operational need
    c. Availability of secure communications
    d. Availability of security storage
    e. All of the above

25. What is the impact of cybersecurity lapses on confidentiality?
a. Data may not be available
b. Data may not be trusted
c. Data may be available to unauthorized persons
d. Users may not be sure of whom they are communicating with
e. Loss of ability to authenticate

26. What is the impact of cybersecurity lapses on integrity?
a. Data may not be available
b. Data may not be trusted
c. Data may be available to unauthorized persons
d. Users may not be sure of whom they are communicating with
e. Loss of ability to authenticate

27. What is the impact of cybersecurity lapses on availability?
a. Data may not be accessible
b. Data may not be trusted
c. Data may be available to unauthorized persons
d. Users may not be sure of whom they are communicating with
e. Loss of ability to authenticate

28. What is the impact of cybersecurity lapses on non-repudiation?
a. Data may not be available
b. Data may not be trusted
c. Data may be available to unauthorized persons
d. Users may not be sure of whom they are communicating with
e. Loss of ability to authenticate

29. Which is true of system categorization?
a. Security personnel should consider impact of information, physical, personal and operational security environment
b. IA controls are selected based upon confidentiality alone
c. Categorizations requires determination of impact of confidentiality, integrity, and availability
d. A. and c.
e. None of the above

30. Which is true of a data spill?
a. Unclassified information is introduced to a classified system
b. Unclassified information is introduced to an accredited system
c. If no unauthorized disclosure occurred, then treat as no compromise
d. Classified information is introduced to an unclassified system
e. None of the above

31. Which is true of data spill reporting?
a. Implement technical isolation
b. Destroy the system
c. Determine whether incident has occurred
d. A. and c.
e. None of the above

32. Which of the following are minimum security requirements for non-traditional work environments?
a. Request for a crime survey where applicable
b. Secure storage of classified material is provided
c. Application of single layer security
d. A. and b.
e. A. and c.

33. Which of the following are risk management roles of the security professional in managing risks associated with new technology and equipment?
a. Understand that technology rarely changes
b. Security managers aren't required to identify new risks
c. Data storage products are not changing as often as they used to
d. Security managers should not recommend policy changes
e. None of the above

34. Which of the following is true of the proper use of social networking services?
   a. Protection of CUI is the same as with other media
   b. Protection of classified information is the same as with other media
   c. Penalties for ignoring requirements are the same as with other media
   d. Governance of social media includes both authorized and unauthorized use
   e. All of the above

35. Which of the following are approved for the storage of confidential classified material?
   a. Requires supplemental controls
   b. Requires GSA approved container
   c. Requires GSA approved container with supplemental controls
   d. B. and c.
   e. None of the above

36. Which of the following is the approval authority for vaults and security containers?
   a. GCA
   b. GSA
   c. CSO
   d. CSA
   e. GTO

37. Which of the following are not authorized for the construction of vaults to protect classified information?
   a. Poured in place concrete
   b. GSA Approved modular vault
   c. Steel lined vault
   d. A. and b.
   e. None of the above

38. Which is identified to serve as the principal point of contact on counterintelligence (CI) and security investigative matters?
a. WHS
b. DTIC
c. DoD CIO
d. Undersecretary of Defense
e. USD (I&S)

39. Which of the following meet standards for secure rooms?
a. Roofs may be constructed of metal panels
b. Doors should be constructed of wood
c. Floors may be constructed of wood
d. Ceilings may be constructed of gypsum
e. All of the above

40. Which of the following are IDS system functions?
a. Detection
b. Communication
c. Assessment
d. Response
e. All of the above

41. Which of the following is recognized as authorized methods to confirm access to a secure area?
a. Visual Control
b. Automated Entry Control System
c. PIN
d. ID badge
e. All of the above

42. In which of the following situations could sanctions be imposed?
a. Disclose CUI to unauthorized persons
b. Classify the classification of information in violation of this Volume
c. Violate any other provision of DoDM 5200.01

d. Continue a SAP contrary to the requirements of this Volume
e. All of the above)

43. Which of the following are potential sanctions for violating provisions of DoDM 5200.01?
a. A warning
b. Forfeiture of pay
c. Loss of right to vote
d. A. and b.
e. All of the above

44. Which of the following are potential sanctions for violating provisions of DoDM 5200.01?
a. Punishment under UCMJ
b. Forfeiture of pay
c. Loss of citizenship
d. A. and b.
e. All of the above

45. Which cover sheet is appropriate for Top Secret information?
a. SF 701
b. SF 702
c. SF 703
d. SF 704
e. SF 705

46. Which cover sheet is appropriate for Confidential information?
a. SF 701
b. SF 702
c. SF 703
d. SF 704
e. SF 705

47. Which label is appropriate for identifying Confidential information on an IT system?
   a. SF 704
   b. SF 705
   c. SF 706
   d. SF 707
   e. SF 708

48. Which classification considerations are associated the Patent Secrecy Act of 1952?
   a. Secretary of Defense may determine that a patent disclosure could cause damage to national security
   b. When the patent contains classified information it shall be protected according to classification level
   c. If patent contains CUI it must be protected accordingly
   d. All of the above
   e. b and d only

49. Which label is appropriate for identifying Unclassified information on an IT system?
   a. SF 706
   b. SF 707
   c. SF 708
   d. SF 709
   e. SF 710

50. Which of the following is a consideration for developing a tetragraph?
   a. Must be three alphabetic characters
   b. Must be four alphabetic characters
   c. Associated membership list must change frequently
   d. Foreign disclosure
   e. B. and d.

51. Which of the following is a consideration for developing a tetragraph?
a. Must be four alphabetic characters
b. Associated membership list must not change frequently
c. Foreign disclosure
d. Impacts to information systems
e. All of the above

52. The purpose of a classification marking is to:
a. Alert to the presence of classified information
b. Provide downgrading guidance
c. Provide declassification guidance
d. Give sources of classification
e. All of the above

53. Which of the following are correct concerning classification markings?
a. The holder or user of the classified information should determine the proper classified information independently of the OCA
b. The highest level of classified information shall not be overly distinguished or stand out on a document
c. The responsibility for marking classified information belongs to the recipient of the information
d. A. and c.
e. None of the above

54. Which of the following are not correct concerning classification markings?
a. The highest level of classified information shall be distinguished or stand out on a document
b. The responsibility for marking classified information belongs to the OCA or author
c. The holder or user of the classified information should determine the proper classified information independently of the OCA
d. A and c
e. All of the above

55. Which is the correct way to redesignate international organization documents marked Restricted?
   a.   UNCLASSIFIED-Modified Handling
   b.   CONTROLLED UNCLASSIFIED INFORMATION-Modified Handling
   c.   CONFIDENTIAL-Modified Handling
   d.   SECRET-Modified Handling
   e.   TOP SECRET-Modified Handling

56. Which is correct concerning Joint Classification Markings?
   a.   Used on information owned by more than one country
   b.   CO-CLASSIFIED should appear on the banner
   c.   Countries of origin are not to be listed in the banner line
   d.   Classified marking should begin with "/"
   e.   None of the above

57. Which are the correct SCI control systems?
   a.   HCS
   b.   SI
   c.   TK
   d.   B. and c.
   e.   All of the above

58. Which is correct concerning the use of NOFORN?
   a.   Should be used with information at the Secret or above levels
   b.   Should be used with information at Confidential or above levels
   c.   Should be reserved for Intelligence documents only
   d.   A. and b.
   e.   None of the above

59. Which is correct concerning the use of NOFORN?
   a.   Should be used with information at the Secret or above levels
   b.   Should be used with information at Confidential or above levels
   c.   Should be used with HCS

d.   Must be used with TK-GEOCAP

e.   None of the above

60.  Of the following, which SAP control markings are interchangeable (either / or)?

I.    Level of classification

II.   Special Access Required

III.  SAR

IV.   Program nickname

V.    Code word

VI.   Dissemination control if assigned

a.   I and II

b.   II and III

c.   I and IV

d.   IV and V

e.   None of the above

61.  Of the following, which SAP control markings are required?

a.   Level of classification

b.   Special Access Required

c.   Program nickname or code word

d.   A. and c.

e.   All of the above

62.  Which is not true of FGI markings?

a.   Used in foreign controlled products with presence of US information

b.   Used in US products with presence of foreign controlled information

c.   Used based on treaties

d.   Used based on agreements

e.   All of the above)

63. Which is true of FGI markings?
a. Used based on agreements
b. Prevents premature declassification
c. Used in US products with presence of foreign controlled information
d. Used in addition to country codes
e. All of the above

64. Which of the following is true concerning ORCON or ORIGINATOR CONTROLLED as used in classification markings?
a. When dissemination requires originator's consent
b. Should be used as often as necessary to limit information sharing
c. Authorized for use by Cleared Defense Contractors
d. May not be used with national intelligence
e. May not be disseminated to contractors within the recipient government facility

65. Which DoDM 5200.01 Volume would you research to find information about the DoD Information Security Program concerning marking of classified information?
a. Volume 2
b. Volume 1
c. Volume 3
d. Volume 4
e. None of the above

66. Which of the following is NOT true concerning ORCON or ORIGINATOR CONTROLLED as used in classification markings?
a. Should be used as often as necessary to limit information sharing
b. Authorized for use by Cleared Defense Contractors
c. May not be used with national intelligence
d. May not be disseminated to contractors within the recipient government facility
e. All of the above

67. Which of the following are true concerning ORCON or ORIGINATOR CONTROLLED as used in classification markings?

    a.   Should be used as often as necessary to limit information sharing

    b.   Not authorized for use by Cleared Defense Contractors

    c.   May be disseminated to contractors within the recipient government facility

    d.   May be used with national intelligence

    e.   All of the above

68. Information may not be designated CUI under which of the following?

    a.   Conceal violations of law

    b.   Conceal inefficiency

    c.   Conceal an administrative error

    d.   Prevent embarrassment

    e.   All of the above

69. Information may be designated CUI under which of the following?

    a.   Restrain competition

    b.   Delay release of information

    c.   Prevent release of information

    d.   Conceal an administrative error

    e.   None of the above

70. In which situation shall information be designated CUI?

    a.   To avoid classification

    b.   To prevent classification

    c.   To require access controls

    d.   To support doubt in the need for classification

    e.   None of the above

71. When is additional CUI education required?
    a. Where individuals review information for public release
    b. Where individuals are involved in acquisition programs
    c. Where individuals are involved in international programs
    d. Where individuals share CUI with outside organizations
    e. All of the above

72. How often is refresher training required for individuals with access to CUI?
    a. Annually
    b. Bi-annually
    c. Semi-annually
    d. Every three years
    e. Continuously

73. Which of the following should be addressed in CUI refresher training?
    a. The importance of classified information
    b. Changes in 5200.01 V1-3
    c. Threats to DoD CUI
    d. B. and c.
    e. None of the above

74. Which of the following should be addressed in CUI refresher training?
    a. The importance of CUI
    b. Changes in 5200.01 V4
    c. Threats to DoD CUI
    d. B. and c.
    e. All of the above

75. Who should receive security management and oversight briefings?
    a. All employees
    b. Security managers
    c. Classification management officers

    d.   B. and c.

    e.   All of the above

76. Which elements should be part of a security termination briefing?

    a.   Reporting unauthorized attempts to access classified information

    b.   Responsibility to submit writings for security review

    c.   Emphasize responsibility to protect classified information

    d.   Responsibility to protect CUI

    e.   All of the above

77. How might a cleared contractor mark unclassified training material to simulate SECRET?

    a.   Unclassified Sample

    b.   Secret For Training Purposes

    c.   Secret For Training Only

    d.   Unclassified – Classified Markings for Training Purposes Only

    e.   All of the above

78. Initial Security Briefings should include which of the following?

    a.   Define classified information

    b.   Define CUI

    c.   Produce a basic understanding of security principles

    d.   A. and c.

    e.   e. All of the above

79. All of the following are portion markings that one might find on foreign classified information EXCEPT:

    a.   TOP SECRET

    b.   SECRET

    c.   REGISTERED)

    d.   RESTRICTED or In Confidence

    e.   UNCLASSIFIED

80. TOP SECRET material shall be stored in:
a. GSA approved security container
b. Approved vault
c. Approved open storage area with supplemental controls
d. A. and c.
e. All of the above

81. Refresher security training for cleared employees must be completed at least:
a. Every six months
b. Annually
c. Quarterly
d. Every three months
e. Upon discretion of FSO

82. Which of the following are part of "DoD Components"?
a. Department of Justice
b. FBI
c. CIA
d. Combatant Commands
e. All of the above

83. How often are employees who conduct derivative classification required to receive derivative classifier training:
a. Annually
b. Semiannually
c. Every two years
d. Once
e. On a case-by-case basis

84. Which is not a responsibility of USD(I&S) concerning advising the Secretary of Defense on the DoD Insider Threat Program?
a. Provide oversight of the DoD Insider Threat Program.
b. Assign responsibilities to the DoD Components to implement the DoD Insider Threat Program.
c. Recommend improvements to the Secretary of Defense on

DoD insider threat activities.
- d. Integrate insider threat activities into national and local policy
- e. None of the above

85. Which of the below should be consulted concerning to access to RD, FRD, and CNWDI within the DoD?
- a. NISPOM
- b. DoDM 5200.01
- c. DoDI 5200.44
- d. DoDI 5210.02
- e. DoDI 5000.83

86. Critical Nuclear Weapon Design Information is a _____ category of SECRET Restricted Data or TOP SECRET Restricted Data.
- a. DOE
- b. DoD
- c. NRC
- d. CSA
- e. DOT

# TEST 3

1. What is the scope of the DoD Information Security Program?
   a. Implements References (b), (d), and (f) with regard to the classification only
   b. Implements References (c), (e), and (g) with regard to the declassification only
   c. Implements References (b), (d), and (f) with regard to the classification, declassification, and protection of classified information
   d. Implements References (c), (e), and (g) with regard to the classification, declassification, and protection of classified information
   e. Implements References (c), (e), and (g) with regard to the implementation of cybersecurity

2. Which of the following is the retention policy for controlled unclassified information?
   a. Shall be maintained only when it is required for effective and efficient operation of the organization
   b. Shall be maintained if law requires its retention
   c. Shall be maintained if treaty requires its retention
   d. Shall be maintained if international agreement requires its retention
   e. All of the above

3. Which classification considerations are associated with information released through the Freedom of Information Act (FOIA)?
   a. There are none as FOIA overrides classification
   b. Classified information is exempt from FOIA processes
   c. The OCA should provide a description of damage with consideration to any FOIA request
   d. A. and c.
   e. A. and b.

4. Of the following, which SAP control markings are optional?
   a. Level of classification
   b. Special Access Required
   c. Program nickname
   d. Code word
   e. Dissemination control

5. Which classification considerations are associated with non-government research and development information?
   a. The government activity shall issue guidance when protection under classification system is requested
   b. The government must determine whether or not those conducting the R&D effort have clearances
   c. If individuals conducting R&D refuse security clearances then the information may not be classified
   d. All of the above
   e. b and d

6. Which of the following are not true about need to know?
   a. An official determination for blanket access to all classified information for a lawful and authorized governmental function
   b. All government employees have need to know
   c. All program managers have need to know of all aspects of their project
   d. Determined primarily by rank and position
   e. All of the above

7. What is the definition of access pertaining to protecting classified information?
   a. The right to access classified information
   b. The desire to access classified information
   c. The acceptance of classified information
   d. The opportunity to access classified information
   e. All of the above

8. Which of the following are identified as authorities for declassification?
   a. Supervisory officials of the OCA if granted authority
   b. Officials designated by DoD component heads
   c. NSA/CSS
   d. A. and c.
   e. All of the above

9. What are the requirements for protecting CNWDI?
   a. Can be emailed to anyone with the appropriate clearance and need to know
   b. Can be emailed to only those who have clearances, need to know and received additional briefings
   c. CNWDI information does not require password protection
   d. Systems containing CNWDI do not need certification
   e. A. and c.

10. Which policies are referred to for protecting SAP information?
    a. Reference (q)
    b. Reference (at)
    c. DoDM 5200.01-V1
    d. B. and c.
    e. All of the above

11. What are tetragraphs?
    a. Used to identify country names
    b. Used to identify international organizations
    c. Used to identify international alliances
    d. B. and c.
    e. All of the above

12. Which is correct concerning the use of NOFORN?
    a. Must be used with HCS
    b. Must be used with TK-GEOCAP
    c. Should be reserved for Intelligence documents only
    d. A. and b.
    e. All of the above

13. Which of the following are authorized dissemination markings?
    a. FOR SHOW
    b. FOR DISPLAY
    c. CONTROLLED INFORMATION
    d. NOT AUTHORIZED FOR RELEASE
    e. DISPLAY ONLY

14. Which are the requirements for protecting open storage classified materials at the TOP SECRET level?
    a. A senior official determines that security in depth is provided
    b. A cleared employee will inspect area during four hour periods
    c. An IDS response team should arrive within 30 minutes of alarm
    d. All of the above
    e. None of the above

15. Which is not an access requirement for Secret?
    a. Non-disclosure agreement
    b. Confidential security clearance Badge card
    c. Need to know
    d. Secret security clearance
    e. All of the above

16. Which is a specific requirement for access to Special Access Programs (SAP)?
    a. SCI-Non-disclosure agreement
    b. Top Secret security clearance
    c. Need to know

    d.   Secret security clearance

    e.   DoD-approved program indoctrination

17.  Who has the authority to originally classify information?
    a.   Prime contractor
    b.   Government employees regardless of position
    c.   Individual authorized in writing to do so
    d.   A. and c.
    e.   All of the above

18.  Which information is not found within a Security Classification Guide?
    a.   Specific items of information to be protected
    b.   Specific classification of information
    c.   Specific reason for classification
    d.   State declassification instructions
    e.   Estimated cost of protecting classified information

19.  Which is a classification duration option for originally classified information?
    a.   A date or independently verifiable event less than 10 years from the date of original classification
    b.   A date 10 years from the date of original classification
    c.   A date 25 years from the date of original classification
    d.   A date or independently verifiable event greater than 10 and less than 25 years from the date of original classification
    e.   All of the above

20.  Which are the authorized methods for the transmission / transportation of Secret classified information?
    a.   U.S. Postal Service standard mail
    b.   U.S. Postal Service certified mail
    c.   Commercial carrier, but no requirement for surveillance service
    d.   On U.S. ships, but no receipt or agreement is necessary
    e.   None of the above

21. Which are general requirements governing the transfer of classified information or material to Foreign Governments?
    a. Transfers shall be conducted through contractor to contractor channels
    b. Letters of Agreement require detailed transfer instructions
    c. Recipients must be designated by recipient government
    d. A. and b.
    e. B. and c.

22. What are the attributes of integrity as it relates to information security?
    a. Ensure that data remains available
    b. Ensure that data remains trusted
    c. Ensure data remains unavailable to unauthorized persons
    d. Ensure users know who they are communicating with
    e. Loss of ability to authenticate

23. Which label is appropriate for identifying Secret information on an IT system?
    a. SF 704
    b. SF 705
    c. SF 706
    d. SF 707
    e. SF 708

24. Which purposes and basic concepts are involved in properly preparing Top Secret materials for transportation?
    a. Outer wrapper must not have individual's name
    b. Outer wrapper must not indicate classification level
    c. A briefcase may serve as an outer wrapper
    d. Specialized shipping containers may serve as outer wrapper
    e. All of the above

25. Which of the following is not a step in the derivative classification process?
    a. Determine if information contains classified information
    b. Derived information should be portion marked
    c. Determine the duration of classification
    d. Contact the originator of classified document or consult the explanation
    e. None of the above

26. Which actions are authorized for hand carrying classified materials?
    a. The information is already available at the delivery address
    b. The lack of operational necessity exists
    c. There are secure communications available
    d. Arrangements have been made for security storage
    e. All of the above

27. What is the impact of cybersecurity lapses on confidentiality?
    a. Data may not be available
    b. Data may not be trusted
    c. Data may be available to unauthorized persons
    d. Users may not be sure of whom they are communicating with
    e. Loss of ability to authenticate

28. What is the impact of cybersecurity lapses on non-repudiation?
    a. Data may not be available
    b. Data may not be trusted
    c. Data may be available to unauthorized persons
    d. Users may not be sure of whom they are communicating with
    e. Loss of ability to authenticate

29. Which is true of system categorization?
    a.  Some systems may need to be categorized depending on risk level
    b.  Depending on risk level, some IA controls may be assigned to systems
    c.  IA controls are selected based upon confidentiality alone
    d.  A. and c.
    e.  None of the above

30. Which is true of a data spill?
    a.  Unclassified information is introduced to a classified system
    b.  Unclassified information is introduced to an accredited system
    c.  If no unauthorized disclosure occurred, then treat as no compromise
    d.  Classified information is introduced to an unclassified system
    e.  None of the above

31. Which is true of data spill reporting?
    a.  Preserve evidence
    b.  Contain to minimize damage
    c.  Evidence may be used for risk assessment
    d.  Evidence may be used for damage assessment
    e.  All of the above

32. Which of the following are identified as minimum security requirements for non-traditional work environments?
    a.  Vocal approval for use of classified material
    b.  Application of single layer security
    c.  Secure storage of classified material is provided
    d.  Self-validation of security review
    e.  None of the above

33. Which of the following are risk management roles of the security professional in managing risks associated with new technology and equipment?
    a. Understand that technology changes frequently
    b. Data storage products are increasingly changing
    c. IT peripherals bring challenges to information security
    d. Security managers should use chain of command to recommend policy changes
    e. All of the above

34. Which of the following is true of the proper use of social networking services?
    a. Use of social media is governed by DoDI 5200.44
    b. Use of social media is governed by DoDM 5000.02
    c. Use of social medica is governed by DoDI 8170.01
    d. Use of social media is governed by DoDM 8150.01
    e. Use of social media is governed by DoDI 8150.01

35. Which of the following are approved for the storage of Secret classified material?
    a. GSA approved security container
    b. In open storage with supplementary controls
    c. Same manner as with Top Secret material
    d. A. and c.
    e. All of the above

36. Which of the following are approved for the storage of confidential classified material?
    a. Requires supplemental controls
    b. Requires GSA approved container
    c. Requires GSA approved vault with supplemental controls
    d. Requires GSA approved container with supplemental controls
    e. B. and c.

37. Which of the following is the correct approval authority for vaults?
    a. GCA
    b. GSA
    c. CSO
    d. CSA
    e. GTO

38. Which of the standards are not authorized for the construction of vaults to protect classified information?
    a. Class C
    b. Class A
    c. Class B
    d. All of the above
    e. None of the above

39. Which of the following do not meet standards for secure rooms?
    a. Walls may be of temporary construction
    b. Doors should be constructed of wood
    c. Floors may be constructed of wood
    d. Roofs may be constructed of metal panels
    e. Ceilings may be constructed of gypsum

40. IDS consists of which of the following?
    a. Intrusion and detection equipment
    b. Intrusion and denial equipment
    c. Denial and detection equipment
    d. Operating forces
    e. None of the above

41. Which are recognized as authorized use of biometric controls for access to a secure area?
    a. Guard
    b. Fingerprints
    c. Keycard

    d.   Lock

    e.   All of the above

42. What is the scope of the DoD Information Security Program?

    a.   Implements References (b), (d), and (f) with regard to the classification only

    b.   Implements References (c), (e), and (g) with regard to the declassification only

    c.   Implements References (b), (d), and (f) with regard to the classification, declassification, and protection of classified information

    d.   Implements References (c), (e), and (g) with regard to the classification, declassification, and protection of classified information

    e.   Implements References (c), (e), and (g) with regard to the implementation of cybersecurity

43. Which statement best describes a security infraction?

    a.   Failure to comply with security requirements

    b.   Security incident resulting in compromise of classified information

    c.   Security incident that does not constitute a violation

    d.   A. and c.

    e.   None of the above

44. What are the characteristics of an investigation?

    a.   Conducted when incident cannot be resolved through inquiry

    b.   Conducted to determine if there is a loss of classified information

    c.   Conducted to determine if classified information was disclosed in an unauthorized manner

    d.   Conducted when a security violation where in-depth examination is required

    e.   All of the above

45. When are administrative controls required?
    a.  When personnel controls are insufficient
    b.  When physical controls are insufficient
    c.  When technical controls are insufficient
    d.  A. and c.
    e.  All of the above

46. Which are the requirements for protecting open storage classified materials at the TOP SECRET level?
    a.  A senior official determines that security in depth is provided
    b.  A cleared employee will inspect area during four hour periods
    c.  An IDS response team should arrive within 30 minutes of alarm
    d.  All of the above
    e.  None of the above

47. Which of the following statements are most accurate as described for the destruction of classified documents/materials?
    a.  Burning, crosscut shredding, wet pulping, chemical decomposition, pulverizing
    b.  Burning, mutilating, pulverizing, chemical decomposition, wet pulping
    c.  Burning, wet pulping, crosscut shredding
    d.  Burning, crosscut shredding, mutilation, wet pulping, chemical decomposition, pulverizing
    e.  Burning, crosscut shredding, wet pulping, chemical decomposition, crushing

48. Which of the following constitute a primary reason(s) to reproduce TOP SECRET documents?
    a.  As required by operational needs
    b.  When directed by FSO
    c.  When directed by CSA
    d.  Contract is renewed
    e.  All of the above

49. Which response time is correct for Top Secret open storage areas with security in depth from the time of alarm announcement?

a. Three minutes
b. Fifteen minutes
c. Five minutes
d. Twenty minutes
e. Thirty minutes

50. Which response time is correct for Top Secret open storage areas without security in depth from the time of alarm announcement?

a. Three minutes
b. Fifteen minutes
c. Five minutes
d. Twenty minutes
e. Thirty minutes

51. Which is identified as the senior official responsible for the portion of the manual pertaining to DoD Information Security Program pertaining to foreign government information?

a. DoD CIO
b. USD
c. Undersecretary of Defense
d. DTIC
e. WHS

52. Which is identified to direct the use of technical means to prevent unauthorized copying of classified data?

a. DTIC
b. WHS
c. DoD CIO
d. Undersecretary of Defense
e. USD

53. What must a person possess prior to being granted access to classified information?
    a. Appropriate security clearance
    b. Valid security clearance
    c. Need to know
    d. Signed a non-disclosure agreement
    e. All of the above

54. A signed SF 312 is required for which security clearance level?
    a. Confidential
    b. Secret
    c. Top Secret
    d. B. and c.
    e. All of the above

55. Once signed, how long must an SF 312 be retained?
    a. 10 years
    b. 30 years
    c. 20 years
    d. 50 years
    e. Indefinitely

56. Prior to gaining access to SCI information, approved individuals must sign a _____?
    a. DA authorized SCI nondisclosure agreement
    b. DoD authorized SCI nondisclosure agreement
    c. DNI authorized SCI nondisclosure agreement
    d. DoE authorized SCI nondisclosure agreement
    e. None of the above

57. Prior to gaining access to SAP information, approved individuals must sign a _____?
    a. DA authorized SCI nondisclosure agreement
    b. DoD authorized SCI nondisclosure agreement
    c. DNI authorized SCI nondisclosure agreement
    d. DoE authorized SCI nondisclosure agreement

e.   None of the above

58. Which DoDM 5200.01 Volume would you research to find information about the DoD Information Security Program concerning overview, classification and declassification?
   a.   Volume 2
   b.   Volume 1
   c.   Volume 3
   d.   Volume 4
   e.   None of the above

59. Which DoDM 5200.01 Volume would you research to find information about the DoD Information Security Program concerning protection of classified information?
   a.   Volume 2
   b.   Volume 1
   c.   Volume 3
   d.   Volume 4
   e.   None of the above

60. Which DoDM 5200.01 Volume would you research to find information about the DoD Information Security Program concerning Controlled Unclassified Information (CUI)?
   a.   Volume 2
   b.   Volume 1
   c.   Volume 3
   d.   Volume 4
   e.   None of the above

61. Which organization is authorized to declassify COMSEC information?
   a.   NSA/CSS
   b.   DNI
   c.   DoD
   d.   Heads of DoD Components
   e.   All of the above

62. Which of the below should be consulted concerning to distribution of RD, FRD, and CNWDI within the DoD?
    a. DoDI 5210.02
    b. NISPOM
    c. DoDM 5200.01
    d. DoDI 5200.44
    e. DoDI 5000.83

63. Employees shall acknowledge that they have been given a NATO security briefing. Signed acknowledgements shall be:
    a. Stored
    b. Maintained
    c. Shredded
    d. Not provided
    e. Optional

64. Which of the below should be consulted concerning access to and distribution of RD, FRD, and CNWDI within the DoD?
    a. NISPOM
    b. DoDM 5200.01
    c. DoDI 5200.44
    d. DoDI 5000.83
    e. DoDI 5210.02

65. When should CNWDI information be authorized for dissemination through e-mail?
    a. When recipient is confirmed to have final security clearance at appropriate level
    b. When recipient is confirmed to have need to know
    c. When recipient is confirmed to have had the required additional security briefing
    d. A. and b.
    e. All of the above

66. When should RD information be authorized for dissemination through e-mail?
   a.  When recipient is confirmed to have final security clearance at appropriate level
   b.  When recipient is confirmed to have need to know
   c.  When recipient is confirmed to have had the required additional security briefing
   d.  A. and b.
   e.  All of the above

67. What is the impact of cybersecurity lapses on non-repudiation?
   a.  Data may not be available
   b.  Data may not be trusted
   c.  Data may be available to unauthorized persons
   d.  Users may not be sure of whom they are communicating with
   e.  Loss of ability to authenticate

68. Which DoDM 5200.01 provisions may military commanders modify as necessary during military operations?
   a.  Accountability
   b.  Transmission
   c.  Dissemination
   d.  A. and b.
   e.  All of the above

69. Which of the following could be subject to sanctions for violations of DoDM 5200.01?
   a.  Contractor personnel
   b.  Military personnel
   c.  Civilian personnel
   d.  B. and c.
   e.  All of the above

70. In which of the following situations could sanctions be imposed?
   a.  Disclose classified information to unauthorized persons
   b.  Classify the classification of information in violation of this Volume
   c.  Continue the classification of information in violation of this Volume
   d.  Create or continue a SAP contrary to the requirements of this Volume
   e.  All of the above

71. Which is true of data spill reporting?
   a.  Report to the OCA
   b.  Report to the information owner
   c.  Report to the responsible computer incident response organization
   d.  A. and c.
   e.  All of the above

72. Which of the following are identified as minimum security requirements for non-traditional work environments?
   a.  Request for a crime survey were applicable
   b.  Storage of classified information can be modified according to home construction
   c.  Security training for employees
   d.  A. and c.
   e.  B. and c.

73. Which of the following are risk management roles of the security professional in managing risks associated with new technology and equipment?
   a.  Understand that technology changes frequently
   b.  Data storage products rarely change
   c.  IT equipment rarely brings new challenges
   d.  Security managers aren't required to identify new risks
   e.  All of the above

74. Which of the following is true of the proper use of social networking services?
 a. Protection of CUI is not the same as with other media
 b. Protection of classified information is the same as with other media
 c. Penalties for ignoring requirements don't exist for social media
 d. Use of social media is prohibited
 e. Non official use of social media is the only authorized use of social media

75. Which of the following are approved for the storage of Top Secret classified material?
 a. GSA approved security container with supplementary protection
 b. GSA approved vault
 c. No IDS is required if cleared employee inspect container
 d. A. and c.
 e. A. and b.

76. Which of the following is the correct approval authority for security containers?
 a. GCA
 b. CSA
 c. CSO
 d. GSA
 e. GTO

77. Which of the standards are authorized for the construction of vaults to protect classified information?
 a. Class C
 b. Class A
 c. Class B
 d. B. and c.
 e. Classes A-C

78. Which is a responsibility of the Secretary of Energy?
   a. Authority for procedures for information classified under AEA
   b. Authority over access to information classified under AEA
   c. Authority over portions pertaining to information classified as RD
   d. Authority over portions pertaining to information classified as FRD
   e. All of the above

79. What are the construction standards for secure rooms?
   a. Walls may be of temporary construction
   b. Walls should be constructed of plaster or other acceptable material
   c. Floors may be of temporary construction
   d. Roofs should be of temporary construction
   e. All of the above

80. Which of the following is the purpose of intrusion detection systems?
   a. Deter unauthorized access
   b. Deny unauthorized access
   c. Detect unauthorized access
   d. A. and b.
   e. A. and c.

81. Which are recognized as authorized use of visual controls for access to a secure area?
   a. Employee
   b. Fingerprints
   c. ID badge
   d. Key
   e. All of the above

82. Contractors who paraphrase classified information are making
_____ decisions:
   a. Reasons for classification
   b. Security Classification Guidance
   c. Derivative classification
   d. Classification
   e. Classified document

83. U.S. RESTRICTED AND FORMERLY RESTRICTED Data is
marked all EXCEPT:
   a. COSMIC TOP SECRET ATOMAL
   b. NATO RESTRICTED ATOMAL
   c. NATO CONFIDENTIAL ATOMAL
   d. NATO SECRET ATOMAL
   e. None of the above

84. Which are appropriate page markings for a document
classified at the SECRET level?
   a. SECRET, TOP SECRET, SENSITIVE, CONFIDENTIAL
   b. CONFIDENTIAL, SECRET, UNCLASSIFIED
   c. CONFIDENTIAL, FOUO, TOP SECRET
   d. UNCLASSIFIED, FOUO, SENSITIVE
   e. All of the above

85. TOP SECRET control officer shall be designated to _____,
_____, _____TOP SECRET information.
   a. Transmit, maintain access and accountability records for, and
receive
   b. Create, classify, brief, document
   c. Receive, create, classify, disseminate
   d. Request, assign, account, disseminate
   e. Receive, transmit, classify, document

86. Pulping may only be used to destroy these kinds of products:
a. Water soluble material
b. Metal
c. Plastic
d. Rubber
e. Computer

# TEST 4

1. 1. The _____ retains authority over access to intelligence methods and sources.
   a. DNI
   b. FBI
   c. DCSA
   d. CIA
   e. SECDEF
   ?

2. The DoD Components provide classification guidance to licensees, _____, grantees or others who possess DoD classified information.
   a. TAAs
   b. Contractors
   c. Licensors
   d. Scopers
   e. Registrars

3. Which of the following are part of "DoD Components"?
   a. Combatant Commands
   b. Department of Justice
   c. FBI
   d. CIA
   e. All of the above

4. SECRET material may be reproduced in the following scenarios, EXCEPT?
   a. In performance of the organization's mission
   b. In compliance of applicable statutes
   c. Upon closure of contract
   d. In compliance of Directives
   e. None of the above

5.  Visitors to DoD Component facilities shall possess _____and _____.
    a.  Clearance, need to know
    b.  Clearance, ID card
    c.  Authorized tablet, pen
    d.  VAL, authorization
    e.  Clearance, authorization

6.  Which of the following is correct concerning the storage of TOP SECRET material?
    a.  In a GSA approved container with supplementary controls
    b.  Lock must meet FF-L-2740, as long as container is in an area with security in depth
    c.  In an approved vault
    d.  All of the above
    e.  None of the above

7.  SECRET material shall be stored in which of the following scenarios:
    a.  GSA approved security container
    b.  Approved vault
    c.  Open storage (Supplemental controls not necessary)
    d.  A. and b.
    e.  All of the above

8.  Which of the following constitute a primary reason(s) to reproduce confidential documents?
    a.  As required by operational needs
    b.  When directed by FSO
    c.  When directed by CSA
    d.  Contract is renewed
    e.  All of the above

9.  Who determines need to know at classified meetings?
    a.  GCA
    b.  Contract monitor

c. Individual disclosing information
d. Visiting individuals
e. FSA

10. TOP SECRET information can be transmitted by which of the
following methods within the U.S. and its territories:
a. Defense Courier Service, if authorized by GCA
b. A courier cleared at the SECRET level
c. By electrical means over contractor approved secured
communication devices
d. By government vehicle
e. By U.S. Postal Service Registered Mail

11. SECRET information can be transmitted by which of the
following means:
a. Registered mail
b. Cleared commercial carrier
c. Express mail between 50 states
d. Approved cleared contractor employees
e. All of the above

12. Couriers shall ensure all EXCEPT:
a. Information shall not be disclosed in public areas
b. Information remains under continuous protection
c. They possess authorization to store classified in hotel safe
d. Locked briefcase may serve as outer layer
e. None of the above

13. The foreign government designation of RESTRICTED should
be given what level of protection in the U. S. where bilateral security
agreements exist:
a. SECRET
b. TOP SECRET
c. CONFIDENTIAL
d. UNCLASSIFIED
e. FOUO

14. Destruction records are required for:
a. TOP SECRET FGI
b. SECRET
c. CONFIDENTIAL
d. A. and b.
e. All of the above

15. Construction in closed areas should be built of material that:
a. Prevents opening by magnetic pulse
b. Prevents opening by shotgun blast
c. Provides evidence of unauthorized access
d. Protects from bomb blasts
e. A. and c.

16. Vents with openings greater than 96 inches and over _____ inches at smallest measurement shall be protected.
a. 2
b. 6
c. 9
d. 10
e. 18

17. Repairs of approved containers include which of the following procedures:
a. Damaged or altered parts are replaced with manufacturer's replacement
b. Damaged or altered parts replaced with identical cannibalized parts
c. Damaged or altered parts are repaired with other than approved methods if storing SECRET material under supplemental controls until October 1, 2012
d. According to FED STD 809
e. All of the above

18. Concerning FGI markings used in U.S. documents, recommendations for the declassification of NATO classified information should be forwarded to:
   a.  Originating activity
   b.  CSA
   c.  CISSP
   d.  DoD component
   e.  FSCC

19. Verification of a meeting, the attendee's identity is verified by official photographic identification such as:
   a.  Passport
   b.  Contractor ID
   c.  Military ID
   d.  CAC card
   e.  All of the above

20. Which of the following meeting items must be approved by the government?
   a.  Menu
   b.  Seating order
   c.  Announcements
   d.  Slide show background
   e.  Dress code

21. When taking action to downgrade classified information, which organization approves the action?
   a.  GSA
   b.  CSA
   c.  OCA
   d.  FBI
   e.  CSO

104 SFPC Master Exam Prep

22. Which of the following apply to end of day security checks?
a. Perform checks at the close of each working day
b. Perform checks at end of last shift in which classified material was removed for use
c. Not necessary during continuing 24 hour operations
d. A. and c.
e. All of the above

23. Which E.O. provides information on marking classified email?
a. E.O. 12353
b. E.O. 13526
c. E.O. 11257
d. E.O. 13691
e. E.O. 12563

24. Which is a responsibility of the Secretary of Energy?
a. Authority for procedures for information classified under AEA
b. Authority over access to information classified under AEA
c. Authority over portions pertaining to information classified as RD
d. Authority over portions pertaining to information classified as FRD
e. All of the above

25. Which of the following should derivative classifiers accomplish?
a. Be an original classifier
b. Complete derivative classifier training
c. Complete a waiver if derivative classifier training is not available
d. Complete FSO certification training
e. A. and c.

26. Which of the following are appropriate portion markings found on classified documents?
a. SECRET, TOP SECRET, CONFIDENTIAL

b. S, TS, C

c. UNCLASSIFIED, TS, CONFIDENTIAL

d. FSO, TS, C, U

e. All of the above

27. The _____ has authority pertaining to access to intelligence methods and sources.
   a. NSA
   b. DoD
   c. DNI
   d. DOA
   e. GCA

28. Contractors shall report all unauthorized disclosure concerning RD and FRD to the:
   a. DOE
   b. NRC
   c. DoD Component
   d. GCA
   e. FSO

29. Challenges to improperly classified RD/FRD documents should be addressed through the:
   a. DoD Component
   b. CSA
   c. DOE
   d. DoD
   e. NRC

30. Contractors shall not disclose CNWDI to subcontractors without approval of the:
   a. CSA
   b. DoD Component
   c. DOE
   d. NRC
   e. FSO

31. For government sponsored classified meetings at contractor facilities, who is responsible for assuming security jurisdiction?
   a. The cleared contractor
   b. The subcontracted security force
   c. Authorizing government agency
   d. Proprietary guard force
   e. CSA

32. TOP SECRET material shall be stored in a(n):
   a. GSA approved security container
   b. Approved vault
   c. Approved closed area with supplemental controls
   d. a and c
   e. All of the above

33. Which of the following can authorize the removal of Top Secret information for use at home?
   a. Chairman of the Joint Chiefs of Staff
   b. Combatant Commanders
   c. Director of National Intelligence
   d. Secretary of Defense
   e. All of the Above

34. Foreign nationals can participate in classified meetings if authorized by the head of the _____ authorizing the meeting.
   a. U.S. Government Agency
   b. FSO
   c. CSO
   d. Contractor
   e. None of the above

35. Reproduction of foreign TOP SECRET information requires approval of the:
   a. GCA
   b. Originating Government
   c. CSA

d.  State Department

e.  None of the above

36.  Employees on federal installations shall safeguard classified information according to procedures of:

a.  NISPOM

b.  Block 13 of DD Form 254

c.  Host Installation or Agency

d.  CSA

e.  CSO

37.  Who is responsible for providing declassification guidance or notification?

a.  CSA

b.  CSO

c.  GSA

d.  Senior Government Official and OCA

e.  None of the above

38.  The _____ is a foreign official assigned to receive classified information from the U.S. government.

a.  COR

b.  DGR

c.  FSO

d.  GCA

e.  State Department

39.  The _____ determines when foreign nuclear information removed from the RD category can be declassified:

a.  Secretary of Energy

b.  DASD(NM)

c.  NRC

d.  DoD

e.  None of the above

40. The _____ determines when FRD pertaining to defense nuclear information can be declassified:
  a.  Secretary of Energy
  b.  DASD(NM)
  c.  NRC
  d.  DoD
  e.  None of the above

41. Which of the following constitute a primary reason(s) to reproduce SECRET documents?
  a.  As required by operational needs
  b.  When directed by FSO
  c.  When directed by CSA
  d.  Contract is renewed
  e.  All of the above

42. The _____ has agency oversight for implementation of the DoD Information Security Program.
  a.  Secretary of Defense
  b.  Director of FBI
  c.  Defense Security Services
  d.  Director of ISOO
  e.  Cognizant Security Agency

43. Which of the following are part of "DoD Components"?
  a.  DOE
  b.  DOJ
  c.  FBI
  d.  CIA
  e.  Military Departments

44. Which of the following are part of "DoD Components"?
  a.  DOE
  b.  DOJ
  c.  FBI
  d.  CIA

e.  Military Departments

45. Which of the following are part of "DoD Components"?
a.  DOE
b.  Office of the Inspector General of the Department of Defense
c.  DOJ
d.  FBI
e.  CIA

46. Which of the following are part of "DoD Components"?
a.  DOE
b.  DoD Field Activities
c.  DOJ
d.  FBI
e.  CIA

47. Which of the following are part of "DoD Components"?
a.  DOE
b.  Combatant Commands
c.  DOJ
d.  FBI
e.  CIA

48. Which of the following are part of "DoD Components"?
a.  DOE
b.  Office of the Chairman of the Joint Chiefs of Staff
c.  DOJ
d.  FBI
e.  CIA

49. Which of the following are NOT part of "DoD Components"?
a.  DOE
b.  Office of the Chairman of the Joint Chiefs of Staff
c.  Combatant Commands
d.  Office of the Inspector General of the Department of Defense
e.  DoD Field Activities

50. Derivative Classification includes:
a. Incorporated classified information
b. Restated classified information
c. Generate classified information in a new form
d. All of the above
e. B. and c.

51. Which inspection requirement is correct for Secret open storage areas with security in depth?
a. Every five hours
b. Every six hours
c. Every three hours
d. Every twenty hours
e. Every four hours

52. Who ensures reviews are conducted for classification challenges?
a. OCA
b. CSA
c. FSO
d. FBI
e. GSA

53. Required security training and briefing titles for all cleared employees include:
a. Initial orientation and annual refresher training
b. OCA training and annual awareness training
c. Declassification training and annual refresher training
d. OCA training and annual refresher training
e. Initial security briefings, annual, refresher

54. All classified information and material should be marked to clearly convey:
a. Level of classification
b. Portions that contain classified
c. Declassification instructions

d.  Date of origin

e.  All of the above

55. NATO has the following identified levels of security classification EXCEPT:

a.  COSMIC TOP SECRET

b.  NATO SECRET

c.  NATO CONFIDENTIAL

d.  NATO RESTRICTED

e.  NATO TOP SECRET

56. CONFIDENTIAL is approved for transmission by which of the following means?

a.  U.S. Postal Service Priority Mail

b.  U.S. Postal Service First Class Mail

c.  Any commercial overnight delivery company

d.  U.S. Postal Service Certified Mail

e.  All of the above

57. Authorization in writing by the _____ is required for transmission of classified information to a foreign government.

a.  CSA

b.  CSA

c.  FSO

d.  CSA

e.  DSA

58. What should be used as authorization to approve a courier in DD Form 2501?

a.  Identification of an individual's recurrent need to hand-carry

b.  Signature of an appropriate official

c.  Emergency communication procedures

d.  a and b

e.  a. and c.

59. Which government agency has jurisdiction over RD?
   a. NSA
   b. FRD
   c. DNI
   d. CSA
   e. DOE

60. Working papers shall be marked the same as finished documents and at the same classification level. Which answer is correct concerning initial draft date?
   a. Transmitted within the facility
   b. Retained for more than 30 days from creation
   c. Retained for more than 180 days from creation
   d. Retained for more than 120 days from creation
   e. Retained for more than 130 days from creation

61. Classified material may be destroyed by which of the following methods?
   a. Mutilation
   b. Chemical decomposition
   c. Pulverization
   d. Melting
   e. All of the above

62. Need to know is generally based on:
   a. Level of clearance
   b. Block 13 of DD Form 254
   c. Security Classification Guide
   d. Authorized government function
   e. As determined by CSA

63. Which of the following apply to end of day security checks?
   a. Perform checks at the close of each working day
   b. Perform checks at end of last shift in which classified material was removed for use
   c. Not necessary during continuing 24 hour operations

d. A. and c.

e. All of the above

64. What should organizations ensure their derivative classifiers accomplish?
a. Be an original classifier
b. Complete derivative classifier training
c. Complete a waiver if derivative classifier training is not available
d. Complete FSO certification training
e. A. and c.

65. Alternative Compensatory Control Measures include items identified as classified:
a. SECRET
b. CONFIDENTIAL
c. Intelligence
d. TOP SECRET
e. None of the above

66. _____ is a DoD category of TOP SECRET Restricted Data or SECRET Restricted Data that reveals operation of components of a thermonuclear bomb.
a. CNWDI
b. FRD
c. RD
d. NATO
e. EWNDI

67. Water soluble papers shall be destroyed by:
a. Shredding
b. Burning
c. Disintegration
d. Pulping
e. A. b. and c.

68. How shall employees certify that they have received a NATO security briefing?
   a. Orally
   b. Verbally
   c. No acknowledgement is required
   d. No briefing is required
   e. A. and b.

69. Which response time is correct for Secret open storage areas with security in depth from the time of alarm announcement?
   a. Three minutes
   b. Fifteen minutes
   c. Five minutes
   d. Twenty minutes
   e. Thirty minutes

70. Which E.O. covers Classified National Security Information?
   a. E.O. 12353
   b. E.O. 13526
   c. E.O. 11257
   d. E.O. 13691
   e. E.O. 12563

71. Which agency has classification authority of COMSEC information?
   a. NSA
   b. DIA
   c. CIA
   d. DoD
   e. DOE

72. The _____ provides the security classification guides.
   a. FSO
   b. CSA
   c. OCA
   d. DoD

e.  Secretary of Defense

73. The SF 312 must be maintained for how long?
a.  Two years
b.  Twenty years
c.  Eighteen months
d.  Fifty years
e.  Five years

74. Methods of approved refresher training include:
a.  Briefings
b.  Instructional materials
c.  Videos
d.  A. and c.
e.  All of the above

75. Freight forwarders who take custody of classified material must have:
a.  FCL
b.  Adequate space
c.  Proper security level storage capacity
d.  A. and b.
e.  A. and c.

76. TOP SECRET information can be transmitted by which methods:
a.  Direct contact between appropriately cleared persons
b.  Registered mail
c.  Express mail
d.  Carriers listed under NISP
e.  U.S. government contract vehicles

77. TOP SECRET information can be transmitted by which methods:
   a. DCS
   b. Authorized U.S. government agency courier services
   c. Direct contact between appropriately cleared persons
   d. Electronic means over an approved secure communications system
   e. All of the above

78. Which DoD Instruction covers the dissemination of CNWDI?
   a. DoDI 5210.02
   b. DoDI 5200.44
   c. DoDI 5200.39
   d. DoDI 5205.11
   e. None of the above

79. When is a signed receipt required for transmission of CONFIDENTIAL material?
   a. Only when transmitted on U.S. registry ships
   b. Always a requirement
   c. If receipt has errors
   d. A. and c.
   e. All of the above

80. Which label is appropriate for identifying Top Secret information on an IT system?
   a. SF 704
   b. SF 705
   c. SF 706
   d. SF 707
   e. SF 708

81. Information classified as SECRET can be transmitted outside of facility by all means EXCEPT:
    a.  Defense Courier Service, if authorized by GCA
    b.  U.S. Postal Service Registered Mail
    c.  U.S. Postal Service Priority Mail
    d.  Cleared commercial carrier
    e.  Cleared commercial messenger service

82. When wrapping classified material for shipment, the _____ cannot go on the outer label:
    a.  Classification level
    b.  Office code letter
    c.  Office code number
    d.  Directions for routing
    e.  Facility name

83. All of the following must be included in the authorization letter for hand carrying classified material on a commercial aircraft EXCEPT:
    a.  Traveler's Social Security Number
    b.  Full name of individual
    c.  Name of person designated to confirm courier authorization
    d.  Courier card including date of issue and expiration
    e.  Name of official issuing letter

84. Which E.O. provides information on marking classified email?
    a.  E.O. 12353
    b.  E.O. 13526
    c.  E.O. 11257
    d.  E.O. 13691
    e.  E.O. 12563

85. Which best explains the retention policy for classified and controlled unclassified information?

a. Shall be maintained only when it is required for effective and efficient operation of the organization

b. Shall be maintained if a law requires its retention

c. Shall be maintained if a treaty requires its retention

d. Shall be maintained if an international agreement requires its retention

e. All of the above

86. Which cover sheet is appropriate for Confidential information?

a. SF 701
b. SF 702
c. SF 703
d. SF 704
e. SF 705

# PRACTICE TEST ANSWERS

We have provided test answers in long and short versions.

Long Version
If you want to compare your answers and continue your study, review the long version answers. This version provides the answer, plus references the NISPOM location to find your answers.

Short Version
Looking for a quick answer? Just go to the short version and see what the answer is.

# TEST 1 ANSWERS-LONG VERSION

1. Which statement best reflects the purpose of the DoD Information Security Program?
   a. Provides overarching program guidance and direction for the DoD Information Security Program  (DoDM 5200.01 Vol 1 Enclosure 3)
   b. Provides ideas for DoD Information Security Program Implementation
   c. Provides training and resources for DoD Information Security Program
   d. Provides executive direction for all DoD security disciplines
   e. None of the above

2. Which of the following are potential sanctions for violating provisions of DoDM 5200.01?
   a. A warning
   b. Forfeiture of pay
   c. Discharge
   d. A. and b.
   e. All of the above (DoDM 5200.01-V1, Enclosure 3 Paragraph 18)

3. Which of the following is not a policy for the retention of classified information?
   a. Shall be maintained only when it is required for effective and efficient operation of the organization
   b. Shall be maintained only when it is required if law requires its retention
   c. Shall be maintained if treaty requires its retention
   d. Shall be maintained if international agreement requires its retention
   e. All apply (DoDM 5200.01 Vol 1 Enclosure 3, Paragraph 14)

4. How does the term "need-to-know," relate to protecting classified information?

    a. All program managers have need to know of all aspects of their project

    b. Determined primarily by rank and position

    c. An official determination for access to specific classified information for a lawful and authorized governmental function (DoDM 5200.01 Vol 1, Definitions)

    d. An official determination for blanket access to all classified information for a lawful and authorized governmental function

    e. Need to know is an expectation for all government civilians


5. How does the term "access," relate to protecting classified information?

    a. The right to access classified information

    b. The ability to access classified information

    c. The acceptance of classified information

    d. The opportunity to access classified information

    e. B. and d. (DoDM 5200.01 Vol, Definitions)


6. Which is not an access requirement for protecting Confidential information?

    a. Non-disclosure agreement

    b. Confidential security clearance

    c. Need to know

    d. Badge card (DoDM 5200.01 Vol 1, Enclosure 3 Paragraph 12)

    e. All are access requirements


7. Which is not an access requirement for protecting Secret information?

    a. Non-disclosure agreement

    b. Confidential security clearance Badge card (DoDM 5200.01 Vol 1, Enclosure 3 Paragraph 12)

    c. Need to know

    d. Secret security clearance

    e. All are access requirements

8. Which is not an access requirement for protecting Top Secret information?
   a. Non-disclosure agreement
   b. Top Secret security clearance
   c. Need to know
   d. Secret security clearance (DoDM 5200.01 Vol 1, Enclosure 3 Paragraph 12)
   e. All are access requirements

9. Which is a specific requirement for access to Sensitive Compartmented Information (SCI)?
   a. DNI authorized SCI-Non-disclosure agreement (DoDM 5200.01 Vol 1, Enclosure 3 Paragraph 12)
   b. Top Secret security clearance
   c. Need to know
   d. Secret security clearance
   e. All are access requirements

10. Which is a specific requirement for access to Special Access Programs (SAP)?
    a. SCI-Non-disclosure agreement
    b. Top Secret security clearance
    c. Need to know
    d. Secret security clearance
    e. DoD approved program indoctrination (DoDM 5200.01 Vol 1, Enclosure 3 Paragraph 12)

11. Which is a specific requirement for access to NATO information?
    a. SCI-Non-disclosure agreement
    b. Top Secret security clearance
    c. Need to know
    d. Secret security clearance
    e. Written acknowledgment of NATO briefing (DoDM 5200.01 Vol 1, Enclosure 3 Paragraph 12)

12. What is original classification?
a. A first edition classified document from which all subsequent documents are numbered
b. An initial determination that information needs protection against unauthorized disclosure (DoDM 5200.01 Vol 1, Definitions)
c. A derived decision that information needs protection against unauthorized disclosure
d. The very first classified document created post WWII
e. None of the above

13. Who has the authority to originally classify information?
a. Prime contractor
b. Government employees regardless of position
c. Individual authorized in writing to do so (DoDM 5200.01 Vol 1, Definitions)
d. A. and c.
e. All of the above

14. Which is not a step of the original classification process?
a. Determine if information is owned by the U.S. Government
b. Determine if information has not already been classified
c. Determine level of national embarrassment disclosure would create (DoDM 5200.01 Vol 1, Enclosure 4, Paragraph 6)
d. Determine and assign the appropriate level of classification
e. Determine the appropriate duration of classification

15. Which is a role of the Original Classification Authority (OCA) in changing classification level?
a. Any appointed OCA can change classification level regardless of jurisdiction
b. An OCA can change the classification level of a document, but not the portion markings
c. An OCA can update security classification guides (DoDM 5200.01 Vol 1, Enclosure 4, Paragraph 7)
d. An OCA is not permitted to communicate classification level changes

e. An OCA cannot authorize the re-marking of classification level changes

16. Which information is not found within a Security Classification Guide?
a. Specific items of information to be protected
b. Specific classification of information
c. Specific reason for classification
d. State declassification instructions
e. Determine level of national embarrassment disclosure would create (DoDM 5200.01 Vol 1, Enclosure 6, Paragraph 2)

17. Which information is not found within a Security Classification Guide?
a. Specific items of information to be protected
b. Specific classification of information
c. Specific reason for classification
d. State declassification instructions
e. Estimated cost of protecting classified information (DoDM 5200.01 Vol 1, Enclosure 6, Paragraph 2)

18. What is tentative classification?
a. Final classification
b. Derived classified information
c. Classification duration
d. Classification pending approval of an OCA (DoDM 5200.01 Vol 1, Enclosure 6, Paragraph 9)
e. Classified items awaiting input into a Security Classification Guide

19. Which is not a classification duration option?

a. A date or independently verifiable event less than 10 years from the date of original classification

b. A date 10 years from the date of original classification

c. A date 25 years from the date of original classification

d. A date 55 years from the date of original classification (DoDM 5200.01 Vol 1, Enclosure 4, Paragraph 13a)

e. A date or independently verifiable event greater than 10 and less than 25 years from the date of original classification

20. Which is a classification duration option for originally classified information?

a. A date or independently verifiable event less than 10 years from the date of original classification

b. A date 10 years from the date of original classification

c. A date 25 years from the date of original classification

d. A date or independently verifiable event greater than 10 and less than 25 years from the date of original classification

e. All of the above (DoDM 5200.01 Vol 1, Enclosure 4, Paragraph 13a)

21. Which cover sheet is appropriate for Secret information?

a. SF 701

b. SF 702

c. SF 703

d. SF 704 (DoDM 5200.01-V2, Enclosure 2, Paragraph 4)

e. SF 705

22. Which is a classification duration option for originally classified information?

a. A date or independently verifiable event less than 10 years from the date of original classification (DoDM 5200.01 Vol 1, Enclosure 4, Paragraph 13a)

b. A date 7 years from the date of original classification

c. A date 20 years from the date of original classification

d. A date or independently verifiable event greater than 5 and less than 15 years from the date of original classification

e.   "50X1-HUM," designating a duration of up to 75 years from the date of original classification

23. The purpose of declassification instructions is to identify:

a.   A date or independently verifiable event less than 10 years from the date of original classification (DoDM 5200.01 Vol 1, Enclosure 4, Paragraph 13a)

b.   A date 7 years from the date of original classification

c.   A date 20 years from the date of original classification

d.   A date or independently verifiable event greater than 5 and less than 15 years from the date of original classification

e.   "50X1-HUM," designating a duration of up to 75 years from the date of original classification

24. What are the requirements for protecting information under the Patent Secrecy Act of 1952?

a.   The Department of Defense shall handle a patent application on which a secrecy order has been imposed (DoDM 5200.01 Vol 1, Enclosure 4, Paragraph 13a)

b.   All patents from the U.S. Government and contractors should be classified

c.   Patents cannot contain classified information

d.   Department of Justice handles all patents and the protection of patents

e.   Inventions are in the public domain, therefore cannot be classified

25. Which of the following is a consideration for developing a tetragraph?

a.   Must be three alphabetic characters

b.   Must be four alphabetic characters (DoDM 5200.01-V2, Enclosure 2, Paragraph 6)

c.   Must be five alphabetic characters

d.   Must be four alphanumeric characters

e.   Associated membership list must change frequently

26. What are the requirements for protecting Nuclear Command and Control-Extremely Sensitive Information (NC2-ESI)?

a. NC2-ESI information shall be marked, safeguarded, and distributed in accordance with 32CFR Part 117

b. NC2-ESI information shall be marked, safeguarded, and distributed in accordance with DoDM 5200.01 Vol 2

c. NC2-ESI information shall be marked, safeguarded, and distributed in accordance with CJCS Instruction 3231.01B (DoDM 5200.01 Vol 1, Enclosure 3, Paragraph 13f)

d. NC2-ESI information shall be marked, safeguarded, and distributed in accordance with DoDM 5200.01 Vol 1

e. NC2-ESI information shall be marked, safeguarded, and distributed in accordance with DoDM 5200.01 Vol 3

27. Which principles are used when challenging a classification decision?

a. The holder should communicate issue with a security manager or the OCA to bring about any necessary correction

b. The holder may informally question classification

c. The holder should provide a sufficient description of information being challenged

d. A. and c.

e. All of the above (DoDM 5200.01 Vol 1, Enclosure 4, Paragraph 22a)

28. Which of the following is a correct procedure to use when challenging a classification decision?

a. Forward challenges through appropriate channels (DoDM 5200.01 Vol 1, Enclosure 4, Paragraph 22a)

b. Provide a general description of information being challenged

c. Holders should seek approval through their immediate supervisor prior to challenging information

d. Justification is rarely required

e. All of the above

29. Which principles and procedures are used when extending classification duration?

a. OCA immediately notifies all known holders of information (DoDM 5200.01 Vol 1, Enclosure 4, Paragraph 13)

b. OCA notifies the GCA of all changes

c. OCA notifies FSOs of changes

d. No action necessary if within 25 years from date of document's origin

e. Information becomes declassified if no action is taken

30. What is derivative classification?

a. Information classified by an OCA

b. Information copied from an originally classified document

c. Information paraphrased from an originally classified document (DoDM 5200.01 Vol 1, Enclosure 4, Paragraph 10)

d. Information duplicated from an originally classified document

e. Information classified by a contractor

31. Which of the following is not a step in the derivative classification process?

a. Determine if information contains classified information

b. Derived information should be portion marked

c. Determine the duration of classification

d. Contact the originator of classified document or consult the explanation

e. All are steps (DoDM 5200.01 Vol 1, Enclosure 4, Paragraph 12)

32. Which authorized sources of security classification guidance can be used in the derivative classification process?

a. The senior security officer

b. Open source research

c. Contradicting sources

d. All of the above

e. None of the above (DoDM 5200.01 Vol 1, Enclosure 4, Paragraph 12)

33. Which is not among the responsibilities of derivative classifiers in protecting classified information?
    a. Observe and respect the OCA classification determination
    b. Do not identify themselves as a derivative classifier (DoDM 5200.01 Vol 1, Enclosure 4, Paragraph 15)
    c. Use only authorized sources
    d. Use caution when restating information
    e. Take appropriate steps to resolve doubt

34. Which classification considerations are associated with the concept of compilation?
    a. Does not reflect any OCA considerations
    b. Elements do not need to be located where one could consider an association
    c. The final decision of classification of compiled data resides with the holder
    d. Classification by compilation requires an OCA decision (DoDM 5200.01 Vol 1, Enclosure 4, Paragraph 16)
    e. The fact that a lot of information is collocated means that it is classified

35. Classification involving the DoD acquisition process shall conform to which of the following?
    a. DoDD 5000.01
    b. DoDD 5200.44
    c. DoDI 5000.02 (DoDM 5200.01 Vol 1, Enclosure 4, Paragraph 16)
    d. A. and c.
    e. All of the above

36. Which classification considerations are associated with information released to the public?
    a. Information declassified without proper authority remains classified
    b. Information that has been released after declassification can be reclassified under certain circumstances

c.   Classified information that has been released without proper authority remains classified

d.   A. and b.

e.   All of the above (DoDM 5200.01 Vol 1, Enclosure 4, Paragraph 17)


37.   Which classification considerations are associated with information released through the Freedom of Information Act (FOIA)?

a.   There are none as FOIA overrides classification

b.   Classified information is exempt from FOIA processes

c.   The OCA should provide a description of damage with consideration to any FOIA request (DoDM 5200.01 Vol 1, Enclosure 3, Paragraph 13)

d.   A. and c.

e.   A. and b.


38.   Which classification considerations are associated with non-government research and development information?

a.   Products are not eligible for classification

b.   The government must acquire a proprietary interest first

c.   The government has an obligation to classified anything under R&D

d.   The non-government entity developing R&D effort requests control under the classification system

e.   B. and d. (DoDM 5200.01 Vol 1, Enclosure 4, Paragraph 19)


39.   Which classification considerations are associated the Patent Secrecy Act of 1952?

a.   Secretary of Defense may determine that a patent disclosure could cause damage to national security

b.   When the patent contains classified information it shall be protected according to classification level

c.   If patent contains CUI it must be protected accordingly

d.   All of the above (DoDM 5200.01 Vol 1, Enclosure 4, Paragraph 20)

e.   B. and d.

132 SFPC Master Exam Prep

40. Which is identified to be responsible for the overall management, functioning, and effectiveness of the information security program within their respective DoD Component?
   a. WHS
   b. Heads of DoD Components (DoDM 5200.01-V1, Enclosure 2, Paragraph 6)
   c. DoD CIO
   d. Undersecretary of Defense
   e. USD

41. Which of the following are identified as authorities for declassification?
   a. Cognizant OCA
   b. Those who have been delegated declassification authority
   c. NSA/CSS
   d. A. and b.
   e. All of the above (DoDM 5200.01 Vol 1, Enclosure 5, Paragraph 3)

42. Which information is found within a Security Declassification Guide?
   a. Information for an effective review of classified information
   b. Information for an effective declassification of classified information
   c. Information for a reclassification of declassified information
   d. A. and b. (DoDM 5200.01 Vol 1, Enclosure 5, Paragraph 3)
   e. All of the above

43. Which are the requirements for protecting Restricted Data (RD)?
   a. RD can be emailed to anyone with the appropriate clearance and need to know
   b. RD can be emailed to only those who have received additional briefings
   c. RD information must be password protected
   d. Systems containing RD do not need certification

e.   A. and c. (DoDM 5200.01 Vol 1, Enclosure 3, Paragraph 13)

44. Which policies protect SCI?
a.   Applicable national policy
b.   Policies established by DNI and implement DoD issuance
c.   DoDM 5200.01-V1
d.   A. and c.
e.   All of the above (DoDM 5200.01 Vol 1, Enclosure 3, Paragraph 13)

45. Which policies protect SAP information?
a.   Reference (q)
b.   Reference (at)
c.   DoDM 5200.01-V1
d.   B. and c.
e.   All of the above (DoDM 5200.01 Vol 1, Enclosure 3, Paragraph 13)

46. Which policies protect foreign government information (FGI)?
a.   Reference (d)
b.   Reference (u)
c.   DoDM 5200.01-V3
d.   International agreements
e.   All of the above  (DoDM 5200.01 Vol 1, Enclosure 3, Paragraph 13)

47. What are the processes associated with downgrading or upgrading classified information?
a.   Line through old markings (DoDM 5200.01 Vol 2, Enclosure 3, Paragraph 10)
b.   Erase old markings
c.   Destroy declassified items and reproduce new declassified ones
d.   Remove cover pages
e.   All of the above

48. Which are not authorized security classifications?

a. Portion marking indicating C, S, TS (DoDM 5200.01 Vol 2, Enclosure 4, Paragraph 4)

b. Restricted, Secret, Top Secret

c. Confidential, Secret, Top Secret

d. Unclassified, Registered, Secret

e. In Confidence, Secret, Restricted

49. Which elements are required on classified information?

a. Overall classification

b. Office of origin

c. Upgrading instructions

d. Only page and portion markings are required

e. A. and b. (DoDM 5200.01 Vol 2, Enclosure 3, Paragraph 3)

50. Which of the following are authorized dissemination markings?

a. FOR OFFICIAL USE ONLY (DoDM 5200.01 Vol 2, Enclosure 4, Fig 25)

b. FOR SHOW

c. FOR DISPLAY

d. CONTROLLED INFORMATION

e. NOT AUTHORIZED FOR RELEASE

51. Which are control markings?

a. Used in banners

b. Separated by classification level with //

c. May be used multiple times on the same line

d. Identify special control systems

e. All of the above (DoDM 5200.01 Vol 2, Enclosure 3, Paragraph 5)

52. What are trigraphs?

a. Used to identify countries (DoDM 5200.01 Vol 2, Enclosure 3, Paragraph 5)

b. Used to identify international organizations

c.  Used to identify international alliances

d.  A. and c.

e.  All of the above


53.  What are tetragraphs?

a.  Used to identify country names

b.  Used to identify international organizations

c.  Used to identify international alliances

d.  b and c (DoDM 5200.01 Vol 2, Enclosure 3, Paragraph 5)

e.  All of the above


54.  Which statement best describes "unauthorized disclosure?"

a.  Transfer of classified information outside of the United States

b.  Transfer of classified information outside of an organization

c.  Transfer of controlled unclassified information to an unauthorized recipient (DoDM 5200.01 Vol 3, Glossary)

d.  Transfer of controlled unclassified information outside of a facility

e.  None of the above


55.  Which are methods for destruction of non-IT media?

a.  Degaussing

b.  Sanding

c.  Chemical decomposition

d.  Mutilation (DoDM 5200.01 Vol 3, Enclosure 3, Paragraph 17)

e.  All of the above


56.  Which statement best describes a security infraction?

a.  Failure to comply with security requirements

b.  Security incident resulting in compromise of classified information

c.  Security incident that does not constitute a violation

d.  A. and c. (DoDM 5200.01 Vol 3, Enclosure 5, Paragraph 1)

e.  None of the above

57. Which statement best describes a security violation?
a. Failure to comply with security requirements
b. Security incident resulting in compromise of classified information (DoDM 5200.01 Vol 3, Enclosure 5, Paragraph 1)
c. Security incident that does not constitute a violation
d. A.and c.
e. None of the above

58. Which statement best describes a compromise?
a. Failure to comply with security requirements
b. Unauthorized disclosure to an unauthorized person (DoDM 5200.01 Vol 3, Enclosure 5, Paragraph 1)
c. Classified information that cannot be located
d. A. and c.
e. None of the above

59. Which statement best describes a loss?
a. Failure to comply with security requirements
b. Unauthorized disclosure to an unauthorized person
c. Security incident that does not constitute a violation
d. Classified information that cannot be located (DoDM 5200.01 Vol 3, Enclosure 5, Paragraph 1)
e. All of the above

60. Which are the requirements for reporting a security infraction?
a. It requires a full investigation at any occurrence
b. It requires an inquiry at all occurrences
c. Infractions can lead to full investigations
d. A. and c. (DoDM 5200.01 Vol 3, Enclosure 5, Paragraph 1)
e. None of the above

61. Which are the requirements for reporting a security violation?
a. It requires a full investigation at any occurrence (DoDM 5200.01 Vol 3, Enclosure 5, Paragraph 1)
b. It requires an inquiry at all occurrences

c. Infractions can lead to full investigations

d. A. and c.

e. None of the above

62. Which are the characteristics of an inquiry?

a. Fact finding analysis

b. Conducted to determine if there is a loss of classified information

c. Conducted to determine if classified information was disclosed in an unauthorized manner

d. A. and c.

e. All of the above (DoDM 5200.01 Vol 3, Enclosure 5, Paragraph 1)

63. Which are the characteristics of an investigation?

a. Conducted when incident cannot be resolved through inquiry

b. Conducted to determine if there is a loss of classified information

c. Conducted to determine if classified information was disclosed in an unauthorized manner

d. Conducted when a security violation where in-depth examination is required

e. All of the above (DoDM 5200.01 Vol 3, Enclosure 5, Paragraph 1)

64. Control measures for safeguarding classified information against unauthorized access may include which of the following?

a. Personnel

b. Physical

c. Technical

d. A. and c.

e. All of the above (DoDM 5200.01 Vol 3, Enclosure 2, Paragraph 1)

65. When are administrative controls required?
    a. When personnel controls are insufficient
    b. When physical controls are insufficient
    c. When technical controls are insufficient
    d. A. and c.
    e. All of the above (DoDM 5200.01 Vol 3, Enclosure 2, Paragraph 1)

66. Which of the following are examples of administrative controls?
    a. Records of internal distribution of classified information
    b. Records of access to classified information
    c. Records of generation of classified information
    d. Records of inventory of classified information
    e. All of the above (DoDM 5200.01 Vol 3, Enclosure 2, Paragraph 1)

67. Which of the following are some custodial responsibilities of individuals to safeguard classified materials?
    a. Control access to classified information
    b. Practice proper measures for storing classified information
    c. Conduct security clearance investigation
    d. A. and c.
    e. A. and b. (DoDM 5200.01 Vol 3, Enclosure 5, Paragraph 3)

68. Which of the following should be provided during initial orientation?
    a. Definition of classified information
    b. How to conduct security incident investigations
    c. A basic understanding of security policies
    d. A. and b.
    e. A. and c. (DoDM 5200.01 Vol 3, Enclosure 5, Paragraph 3)

69. Which manual addresses security incidents involving Alternative Compensatory Control Measures (ACCM)?
   a.  DoDM 5200.01 Vol 3, Enclosure 2 (DoDM 5200.01 Vol 3, Enclosure 5, Paragraph 3)
   b.  DODM 5200.01 Vol 2, Enclosure 2
   c.  32 CFR Part 117, Paragraph 20
   d.  DoDI 5220.01, Enclosure 3
   e.  DoDM 5400.02

70. Concerning employees outside the executive branch, which of the following statements is false?
   a.  Must be necessary for a lawful use
   b.  Does not need to be permitted by OCA
   c.  Must be necessary for authorized used
   d.  Recipient eligibility should be determined
   e.  None of the above (DoDM 5200.01 Vol 3, Enclosure 2, Paragraph 6)

71. Which are requirements for protecting open storage classified materials at the SECRET level?
   a.  A senior official determines that security in depth is provided
   b.  A cleared employee will inspect area during four hour periods
   c.  An IDS response team should arrive within 30 minutes of alarm
   d.  All of the above (DoDM 5200.01 Vol 3, Enclosure 3, Paragraph 3)
   e.  None of the above

72. Which of the following statements are most accurate as described for the destruction of classified IT?
   a.  Overwriting and degaussing
   b.  Degaussing and sanding
   c.  Sanding and overwriting
   d.  Overwriting, sanding and physical destruction
   e.  Sanding, degaussing, overwriting and physical destruction (DoDM 5200.01 Vol 3, Enclosure 3, Paragraph 17)

73. Which are the authorized methods for the transmission / transportation of Confidential classified information?
a. U.S. Postal Service standard mail
b. U.S. Postal Service registered mail (DoDM 5200.01 Vol 3, Enclosure 4, Paragraph 3)
c. Commercial carrier, but no requirement for surveillance service
d. On U.S. ships, but no receipt or agreement is necessary
e. On any ship with any registry as long as receipts are provided

74. Which are the purposes and basic concepts involved in properly preparing Secret materials for transportation?
a. Outer wrapper must have individuals name
b. Outer wrapper must contain classification level
c. A briefcase may serve as an outer wrapper (DoDM 5200.01 Vol 3, Enclosure 10, Paragraph 3)
d. Specialized shipping containers may not serve as outer wrapper
e. All of the above

75. Which actions are authorized for hand carrying classified materials?
a. The information is already available at the delivery address
b. The lack of operational necessity exists
c. There are secure communications available
d. Arrangements have been made for security storage (DoDM 5200.01 Vol 3, Enclosure 4, Paragraph 12)
e. All of the above

76. Which are general requirements governing the transfer of classified information or material to Foreign Governments?
a. Transfers could occur in the continental U.S.
b. Transfers of classified information only occur outside of the continental U.S.
c. Recipients must be designated by recipient government
d. A. and c. (DoDM 5200.01 Vol 3, Enclosure 4, Paragraph 1)

e.   B. and c.

77.  Which are general requirements governing the transfer of classified information or material to Foreign Governments?
a.   Transfers shall be conducted through contractor to contractor channels
b.   Letters of Agreement require detailed transfer instructions
c.   Recipients must be designated by recipient government
d.   A. and b.
e.   B. and c. (DoDM 5200.01 Vol 3, Enclosure 4, Paragraph 1)

78.  Which are the attributes of confidentiality as it relates to information security?
a.   Ensure that data remains available
b.   Ensure that data remains trusted
c.   Ensure data remains unavailable to unauthorized persons (DoDM 5200.01 Vol 3, Enclosure 7, Paragraph 4)
d.   Ensure users know who they are communicating with
e.   Loss of ability to authenticate

79.  The Director of National Intelligence prescribes the sections of the Manual that address _____ and _____ including _____.
a.   Operations, intelligence sources, procurement
b.   Intelligence sources, methods, SCI ((DoDM 5200.01 Vol 1, Paragraph 2)
c.   SAP, intelligence sources, means
d.   Organization, classification, procurement
e.   Classification, dissemination, intelligence sources

80. Which are the attributes of integrity relating to information security?
a. Ensure that data remains available
b. Ensure that data remains trusted (DoDM 5200.01 Vol 3, Enclosure 7, Paragraph 4)
c. Ensure data remains unavailable to unauthorized persons
d. Ensure users know who they are communicating with
e. Loss of ability to authenticate

81. Which are the attributes of availability relating to information security?
a. Ensure that data remains accessible (DoDM 5200.01 Vol 3, Enclosure 7, Paragraph 4)
b. Ensure that data remains trusted
c. Ensure data remains unavailable to unauthorized persons
d. Ensure users know who they are communicating with
e. Loss of ability to authenticate

82. Which are the attributes of non-repudiation as relating to information security?
a. Ensure that data remains accessible
b. Ensure that data remains trusted
c. Ensure data remains unavailable to unauthorized persons
d. Ensure users know who they are communicating with (DoDM 5200.01 Vol 3, Enclosure 7, Paragraph 4)
e. Loss of ability to authenticate

83. Which are methods for destruction of IT media?
a. Overwriting
b. Sanding
c. Chemical decomposition
d. A. and b. (DoDM 5200.01 Vol 3, Enclosure 3, Paragraph 17)
e. All of the above

84. What is the impact of cybersecurity lapses on confidentiality?
a. Data may not be available
b. Data may not be trusted
c. Data may be available to unauthorized persons (DoDM 5200.01 Vol 3, Enclosure 7, Paragraph 4)
d. Users may not be sure of whom they are communicating with
e. Loss of ability to authenticate

85. What are some characteristics of system categorization?
a. Requires determination of impact of confidence, integration and availability
b. Requires determination of impact of confidence, integrity and availability
c. Requires determination of impact of confidential, secret and top secret
d. Requires determination of impact of confidentiality, integrity, and availability (DoDM 5200.01 Vol 3, Enclosure 7, Paragraph 4)
e. Requires determination of impact of confidentiality, integrity, and availableness

86. Which is true of a data spill?
a. The activity security manager has overall responsibility of network operations
b. The activity security manager ensures policy requirements are met (DoDM 5200.01 Vol 3, Enclosure 7, Paragraph 5)
c. The IA staff ensures policy requirements are met
d. Users have overall responsibility of network operations
e. All of the above

1. Which best describes a purpose or scope of the DoD Information Security Program?
   a. Provides executive direction for all DoD security disciplines with regard to declassification only
   b. Provides overarching program guidance and direction for the DoD Information Security Program with regard to the classification, declassification, and protection of classified information (DoDM 5200.01 Vol 1, Enclosure 3)
   c. Provides ideas for DoD Information Security Program Implementation with regard to the classification, declassification, and protection of classified information
   d. A. and b.
   e. None of the above

2. Which best explains the retention policy for classified and controlled unclassified information?
   a. Shall be maintained only when it is required for effective and efficient operation of the organization
   b. Shall be maintained if a law requires its retention
   c. Shall be maintained if a treaty requires its retention
   d. Shall be maintained if an international agreement requires its retention
   e. All of the above (DoDM 5200.01 Vol 1 Enclosure 3, Paragraph 14)

3. Which document provides DoD policy concerning access to Formerly Restricted Data (FRD)?
   a. DoDI 5210.02 (DoDM 5200.01 Vol 1, Enclosure 3, Paragraph 13)
   b. DoDI 5200.44
   c. DoDM 5200.01
   d. DoDM 5300.02
   e. None of the above

4.  Which provides procedures and minimum security standards for the handling and protection of NATO classified information and was written by USD (P)?
    a.  Reference (d)
    b.  Reference (u) (DoDM 5200.01 Vol 1, Enclosure 2, Paragraph 8)
    c.  DoDM 5200.01-V3
    d.  International agreements
    e.  All of the above

5.  Which is a specific requirement for access to NATO?
    a.  SCI-Non-disclosure agreement
    b.  Top Secret security clearance
    c.  Need to know
    d.  Secret security clearance
    e.  Written acknowledgment of NATO briefing (DoDM 5200.01 Vol 1, Enclosure 3, Paragraph 12)

6.  Which is not a step of the original classification process?
    a.  Determine if information is owned by the U.S. Government
    b.  Determine if information has not already been classified
    c.  Determine level of national embarrassment that disclosure would create (DoDM 5200.01 Vol 1, Enclosure 4, Paragraph 6)
    d.  Determine and assign the appropriate level of classification
    e.  Determine the appropriate duration of classification

7.  Which is a classification duration option for originally classified information?
    a.  A date or independently verifiable event less than 10 years from the date of original classification (DoDM 5200.01 Vol 1, Enclosure 4, Paragraph 13a)
    b.  A date 7 years from the date of original classification
    c.  A date 20 years from the date of original classification
    d.  A date or independently verifiable event greater than 5 and less than 15 years from the date of original classification
    e.  "50X1-HUM," designating a duration of up to 75 years from the date of original classification

8. Which authorized sources of security classification guidance can be used in the derivative classification process?

    a. The OCA

    b. Originator of source document

    c. Security Classification Guides

    d. All of the above (DoDM 5200.01 Vol 1, Enclosure 4, Paragraph 12)

    e. None of the above


9. Which classification considerations are associated the Patent Secrecy Act of 1952?

    a. Secretary of Defense may determine that a patent disclosure could cause damage to national security

    b. When the patent contains classified information it shall be protected according to classification level

    c. If patent contains CUI it must be protected accordingly

    d. All of the above (DoDM 5200.01 Vol 1, Enclosure 4, Paragraph 20)

    e. B. and d.


10. Which of the following are identified as authorities for declassification?

    a. Cognizant OCA

    b. Those who have been delegated declassification authority

    c. NSA/CSS

    d. All of the above (DoDM 5200.01 Vol 1, Enclosure 5, Paragraph 3)

    e. A. and b.


11. Which document provides DoD policy concerning access to Formerly Restricted Data (FRD)?

    a. DoDI 5210.02 (DoDM 5200.01 Vol 1, Enclosure 3, Paragraph 13)

    b. DoDI 5200.44

    c. DoDM 5200.01

    d. DoDM 5300.02

    e. None of the above

12. Which policies are referred to for protecting NATO and FGI information?
    a. Reference (d)
    b. Reference (u)
    c. DoDM 5200.01-V3
    d. International agreements
    e. All of the above (DoDM 5200.01 Vol 1, Enclosure 3, Paragraph 13)

13. Which of the following are authorized dissemination markings?
    a. FOR SHOW
    b. CONTROLLABLE IMAGERY (DoDM 5200.01 Vol 2, Enclosure 4, Fig 25)
    c. FOR DISPLAY
    d. CONTROLLED INFORMATION
    e. NOT AUTHORIZED FOR RELEASE

14. Which of the following is untrue concerning requirements for protecting open storage classified materials at the CONFIDENTIAL level?
    a. A senior official determines that security in depth is provided
    b. A cleared employee will inspect area during four hour periods
    c. An IDS response team should arrive within 30 minutes of alarm (DoDM 5200.01 Vol 3, Enclosure 3, Paragraph 3)
    d. All of the above
    e. None of the above

15. Which is not an access requirement for Top Secret?
    a. Non-disclosure agreement
    b. Top Secret security clearance
    c. Need to know
    d. Secret security clearance (DoDM 5200.01 Vol 1, Enclosure 3, Paragraph 12)
    e. All of the above

16. Which statement best describes a security violation?
a. Failure to comply with security requirements
b. Security incident resulting in compromise of classified information (DoDM 5200.01 Vol 3, Enclosure 5, Paragraph 1)
c. Security incident that does not constitute a violation
d. A. and c.
e. None of the above


17. What are the requirements for reporting a security infraction?
a. It requires a full investigation at any occurrence
b. It requires an inquiry at all occurrences
c. Infractions can lead to full investigations
d. A. and c. (DoDM 5200.01 Vol 3, Enclosure 5, Paragraph 1)
e. None of the above


18. Which of the following are examples of administrative controls?
a. Records of internal distribution of classified information
b. Records of access to classified information
c. Records of generation of classified information
d. Records of inventory of classified information
e. All of the above (DoDM 5200.01 Vol 3, Enclosure 2, Paragraph 1)


19. What are the attributes of availability as it relates to information security?
a. Ensure that data remains accessible (DoDM 5200.01 Vol 3, Enclosure 7, Paragraph 4)
b. Ensure that data remains trusted
c. Ensure data remains unavailable to unauthorized persons
d. Ensure users know who they are communicating with
e. Loss of ability to authenticate

20. Which are the authorized methods for the transmission/transportation of Top Secret classified information?

a. From cleared person to cleared person as long as they have need to know

b. NSA approved electronic means

c. Defense Courier Service

d. DCS approved specialized shipping container

e. All of the above (DoDM 5200.01 Vol 3, Enclosure 4, Paragraph 3)


21. Which of the following are true about need to know?

a. All government employees have need to know

b. All program managers have need to know of all aspects of their project

c. Determined primarily by rank and position

d. An official determination for access to all classified information for a lawful and authorized governmental function

e. An official determination for access to specific classified information for a lawful and authorized governmental function (DoDM 5200.01 Vol 1, Definitions)


22. Which purpose and basic concepts are involved in properly preparing Confidential materials for transportation?

a. Inner wrapper may contain individuals name

b. Inner wrapper must not contain classification level

c. A briefcase may serve as an outer wrapper

d. For classified information that cannot be packaged and the outside is classified, no outer wrapper is necessary

e. A. and c. (DoDM 5200.01 Vol 3, Enclosure 4, Paragraph 10)


23. Which of the following provides the best definition of accessing classified information?

a. The desire to access classified information

b. The acceptance of classified information

c. The opportunity to access classified information (DoDM 5200.01 Vol, Definitions)

d. The right to access classified information

e. All of the above


24. Which of the following is a consideration for hand carrying classified material?

a. The availability at the delivery address

b. Existence of operational need

c. Availability of secure communications

d. Availability of security storage

e. All of the above (DoDM 5200.01 Vol 3, Enclosure 4, Paragraph 12)


25. What is the impact of cybersecurity lapses on confidentiality?

a. Data may not be available

b. Data may not be trusted

c. Data may be available to unauthorized persons (DoDM 5200.01 Vol 3, Enclosure 7, Paragraph 4)

d. Users may not be sure of whom they are communicating with

e. Loss of ability to authenticate


26. What is the impact of cybersecurity lapses on integrity?

a. Data may not be available

b. Data may not be trusted (DoDM 5200.01 Vol 3, Enclosure 7, Paragraph 4)

c. Data may be available to unauthorized persons

d. Users may not be sure of whom they are communicating with

e. Loss of ability to authenticate


27. What is the impact of cybersecurity lapses on availability?

a. Data may not be accessible (DoDM 5200.01 Vol 3, Enclosure 7, Paragraph 4)

b. Data may not be trusted

c. Data may be available to unauthorized persons

d. Users may not be sure of whom they are communicating with

e. Loss of ability to authenticate

152 SFPC Master Exam Prep

28. What is the impact of cybersecurity lapses on non-repudiation?
a. Data may not be available
b. Data may not be trusted
c. Data may be available to unauthorized persons
d. Users may not be sure of whom they are communicating with (DoDM 5200.01 Vol 3, Enclosure 7, Paragraph 4)
e. Loss of ability to authenticate

29. Which is true of system categorization?
a. Security personnel should consider impact of information, physical, personal and operational security environment
b. IA controls are selected based upon confidentiality alone
c. Categorizations requires determination of impact of confidentiality, integrity, and availability
d. A. and c. (DoDM 5200.01 Vol 3, Enclosure 7, Paragraph 4)
e. None of the above

30. Which is true of a data spill?
a. Unclassified information is introduced to a classified system
b. Unclassified information is introduced to an accredited system
c. If no unauthorized disclosure occurred, then treat as no compromise
d. Classified information is introduced to an unclassified system (DoDM 5200.01 Vol 3, Enclosure 7, Paragraph 5)
e. None of the above

31. Which is true of data spill reporting?
a. Implement technical isolation
b. Destroy the system
c. Determine whether incident has occurred
d. A. and c. (DoDM 5200.01 Vol 3, Enclosure 7, Paragraph 5)
e. None of the above

32. Which of the following are minimum security requirements for non-traditional work environments?
   a. Request for a crime survey where applicable
   b. Secure storage of classified material is provided
   c. Application of single layer security
   d. A. and b. (DoDM 5200.01 Vol 3, Enclosure 7, Paragraph 7)
   e. A. and c.

33. Which of the following are risk management roles of the security professional in managing risks associated with new technology and equipment?
   a. Understand that technology rarely changes
   b. Security managers aren't required to identify new risks
   c. Data storage products are not changing as often as they used to
   d. Security managers should not recommend policy changes
   e. None of the above (DoDM 5200.01 Vol 3, Enclosure 7, Paragraph 10)

34. Which of the following is true of the proper use of social networking services?
   a. Protection of CUI is the same as with other media
   b. Protection of classified information is the same as with other media
   c. Penalties for ignoring requirements are the same as with other media
   d. Governance of social media includes both authorized and unauthorized use
   e. All of the above (DoDM 5200.01 Vol 3, Enclosure 7, Paragraph 11)

154 SFPC Master Exam Prep

35. Which of the following are approved for the storage of confidential classified material?
    a. Requires supplemental controls
    b. Requires GSA approved container (DoDM 5200.01 Vol 3, Enclosure 3, Paragraph 3)
    c. Requires GSA approved container with supplemental controls
    d. B. and c.
    e. None of the above

36. Which of the following is the approval authority for vaults and security containers?
    a. GCA
    b. GSA (DoDM 5200.01 Vol 3, Enclosure 3, Paragraph 3)
    c. CSO
    d. CSA
    e. GTO

37. Which of the following are not authorized for the construction of vaults to protect classified information?
    a. Poured in place concrete
    b. GSA Approved modular vault
    c. Steel lined vault (DoDM 5200.01 Vol 3, Appendix to Enclosure 3, Paragraph 1)
    d. A. and b.
    e. None of the above

38. Which is identified to serve as the principal point of contact on counterintelligence (CI) and security investigative matters?
    a. WHS
    b. DTIC
    c. DoD CIO
    d. Undersecretary of Defense
    e. USD (I&S) (DoDM 5200.01-V1, Enclosure 2, Paragraph 1)

39. Which of the following meet standards for secure rooms?
a. Roofs may be constructed of metal panels
b. Doors should be constructed of wood
c. Floors may be constructed of wood
d. Ceilings may be constructed of gypsum
e. All of the above (DoDM 5200.01 Vol 3, Appendix to Enclosure 3, Paragraph 1)

40. Which of the following are IDS system functions?
a. Detection
b. Communication
c. Assessment
d. Response
e. All of the above (DoDM 5200.01 Vol 3, Appendix to Enclosure 3, Paragraph 2)

41. Which of the following is recognized as authorized methods to confirm access to a secure area?
a. Visual Control
b. Automated Entry Control System
c. PIN
d. ID badge
e. All of the above (DoDM 5200.01 Vol 3, Appendix to Enclosure 3, Paragraph 3)

42. In which of the following situations could sanctions be imposed?
a. Disclose CUI to unauthorized persons
b. Classify the classification of information in violation of this Volume
c. Violate any other provision of DoDM 5200.01
d. Continue a SAP contrary to the requirements of this Volume
e. All of the above (DoDM 5200.01-V1, Enclosure 3, Paragraph 18)

43. Which of the following are potential sanctions for violating provisions of DoDM 5200.01?
   a. A warning
   b. Forfeiture of pay
   c. Loss of right to vote
   d. A. and b. (DoDM 5200.01-V1, Enclosure 3 Paragraph 18)
   e. All of the above

44. Which of the following are potential sanctions for violating provisions of DoDM 5200.01?
   a. Punishment under UCMJ
   b. Forfeiture of pay
   c. Loss of citizenship
   d. A. and b. (DoDM 5200.01-V1, Enclosure 3 Paragraph 18)
   e. All of the above

45. Which cover sheet is appropriate for Top Secret information?
   a. SF 701
   b. SF 702
   c. SF 703 (DoDM 5200.01-V2, Enclosure 2, Paragraph 4)
   d. SF 704
   e. SF 705

46. Which cover sheet is appropriate for Confidential information?
   a. SF 701
   b. SF 702
   c. SF 703
   d. SF 704
   e. SF 705 (DoDM 5200.01-V2, Enclosure 2, Paragraph 4)

47. Which label is appropriate for identifying Confidential information on an IT system?
   a. SF 704
   b. SF 705
   c. SF 706
   d. SF 707

e.   SF 708 (DoDM 5200.01-V2, Enclosure 2, Paragraph 4)

48. Which classification considerations are associated the Patent Secrecy Act of 1952?
   a.   Secretary of Defense may determine that a patent disclosure could cause damage to national security
   b.   When the patent contains classified information it shall be protected according to classification level
   c.   If patent contains CUI it must be protected accordingly
   d.   All of the above (DoDM 5200.01 Vol 1, Enclosure 4, Paragraph 20)
   e.   b and d only

49. Which label is appropriate for identifying Unclassified information on an IT system?
   a.   SF 706
   b.   SF 707
   c.   SF 708
   d.   SF 709
   e.   SF 710 (DoDM 5200.01-V2, Enclosure 2, Paragraph 4)

50. Which of the following is a consideration for developing a tetragraph?
   a.   Must be three alphabetic characters
   b.   Must be four alphabetic characters
   c.   Associated membership list must change frequently
   d.   Foreign disclosure
   e.   B. and d. (DoDM 5200.01-V2, Enclosure 2, Paragraph 6)

51. Which of the following is a consideration for developing a tetragraph?
   a.   Must be four alphabetic characters
   b.   Associated membership list must not change frequently
   c.   Foreign disclosure
   d.   Impacts to information systems
   e.   All of the above (DoDM 5200.01-V2, Enclosure 2, Paragraph 6)

52. The purpose of a classification marking is to:
a. Alert to the presence of classified information
b. Provide downgrading guidance
c. Provide declassification guidance
d. Give sources of classification
e. All of the above (DoDM 5200.01-V2, Enclosure 3, Paragraph 1)

53. Which of the following are correct concerning classification markings?
a. The holder or user of the classified information should determine the proper classified information independently of the OCA
b. The highest level of classified information shall not be overly distinguished or stand out on a document
c. The responsibility for marking classified information belongs to the recipient of the information
d. A. and c.
e. None of the above (DoDM 5200.01-V2, Enclosure 3, Paragraph 2)

54. Which of the following are not correct concerning classification markings?
a. The highest level of classified information shall be distinguished or stand out on a document
b. The responsibility for marking classified information belongs to the OCA or author
c. The holder or user of the classified information should determine the proper classified information independently of the OCA (DoDM 5200.01-V2, Enclosure 3, Paragraph 2)
d. A and c
e. All of the above

55. Which is the correct way to redesignate international organization documents marked Restricted?

    a. UNCLASSIFIED-Modified Handling

    b. CONTROLLED UNCLASSIFIED INFORMATION-Modified Handling

    c. CONFIDENTIAL-Modified Handling (DoDM 5200.01-V2, Enclosure 4, Paragraph 4)

    d. SECRET-Modified Handling

    e. TOP SECRET-Modified Handling

56. Which is correct concerning Joint Classification Markings?

    a. Used on information owned by more than one country (DoDM 5200.01-V2, Enclosure 4, Paragraph 5)

    b. CO-CLASSIFIED should appear on the banner

    c. Countries of origin are not to be listed in the banner line

    d. Classified marking should begin with "/"

    e. None of the above

57. Which are the correct SCI control systems?

    a. HCS

    b. SI

    c. TK

    d. B. and c.

    e. All of the above (DoDM 5200.01-V2, Enclosure 4, Paragraph 6)

58. Which is correct concerning the use of NOFORN?

    a. Should be used with information at the Secret or above levels

    b. Should be used with information at Confidential or above levels

    c. Should be reserved for Intelligence documents only (DoDM 5200.01-V2, Enclosure 4 ,Paragraph 6)

    d. A. and b.

    e. None of the above

59. Which is correct concerning the use of NOFORN?
    a. Should be used with information at the Secret or above levels
    b. Should be used with information at Confidential or above levels
    c. Should be used with HCS
    d. Must be used with TK-GEOCAP
    e. None of the above (DoDM 5200.01-V2, Enclosure 4, Paragraph 6)

60. Of the following, which SAP control markings are interchangeable (either / or)?
    I. Level of classification
    II. Special Access Required
    III. SAR
    IV. Program nickname
    V. Code word
    VI. Dissemination control if assigned
    a. I and II
    b. II and III (DoDM 5200.01-V2, Enclosure 4, Paragraph 7)
    c. I and IV
    d. IV and V
    e. None of the above

61. Of the following, which SAP control markings are required?
    a. Level of classification
    b. Special Access Required
    c. Program nickname or code word
    d. A. and c.
    e. All of the above (DoDM 5200.01-V2, Enclosure 4, Paragraph 7)

62. Which is not true of FGI markings?
    a. Used in foreign controlled products with presence of US information
    b. Used in US products with presence of foreign controlled information
    c. Used based on treaties

d. Used based on agreements

e. All of the above (DoDM 5200.01-V2, Enclosure 4, Paragraph 9)

63. Which is true of FGI markings?

a. Used based on agreements

b. Prevents premature declassification

c. Used in US products with presence of foreign controlled information

d. Used in addition to country codes

e. All of the above (DoDM 5200.01-V2, Enclosure 4, Paragraph 9)

64. Which of the following is true concerning ORCON or ORIGINATOR CONTROLLED as used in classification markings?

a. When dissemination requires originator's consent (DoDM 5200.01-V2, Enclosure 4, Paragraph 10)

b. Should be used as often as necessary to limit information sharing

c. Authorized for use by Cleared Defense Contractors

d. May not be used with national intelligence

e. May not be disseminated to contractors within the recipient government facility

65. Which DoDM 5200.01 Volume would you research to find information about the DoD Information Security Program concerning marking of classified information?

a. Volume 2 (DoDM 5200.01-V2)

b. Volume 1

c. Volume 3

d. Volume 4

e. None of the above

66. Which of the following is NOT true concerning ORCON or ORIGINATOR CONTROLLED as used in classification markings?

a. Should be used as often as necessary to limit information sharing

b. Authorized for use by Cleared Defense Contractors

c. May not be used with national intelligence

d. May not be disseminated to contractors within the recipient government facility

e. All of the above (DoDM 5200.01-V2, Enclosure 4, Paragraph 10)

67. Which of the following are true concerning ORCON or ORIGINATOR CONTROLLED as used in classification markings?

a. Should be used as often as necessary to limit information sharing

b. Not authorized for use by Cleared Defense Contractors

c. May be disseminated to contractors within the recipient government facility

d. May be used with national intelligence

e. All of the above (DoDM 5200.01-V2, Enclosure 4, Paragraph 10)

68. Information may not be designated CUI under which of the following?

a. Conceal violations of law

b. Conceal inefficiency

c. Conceal an administrative error

d. Prevent embarrassment

e. All of the above (DoDM 5200.01-V4, Enclosure 3, Paragraph 1)

69. Information may be designated CUI under which of the following?

a. Restrain competition

b. Delay release of information

c. Prevent release of information

d. Conceal an administrative error

e.  None of the above (DoDM 5200.01-V4, Enclosure 3, Paragraph 1)

70.  In which situation shall information be designated CUI?
a.  To avoid classification
b.  To prevent classification
c.  To require access controls (DoDM 5200.01-V4, Enclosure 3, Paragraph 1)
d.  To support doubt in the need for classification
e.  None of the above

71.  When is additional CUI education required?
a.  Where individuals review information for public release
b.  Where individuals are involved in acquisition programs
c.  Where individuals are involved in international programs
d.  Where individuals share CUI with outside organizations
e.  All of the above (DoDM 5200.01-V4, Enclosure 3, Paragraph 1)

72.  How often is refresher training required for individuals with access to CUI?
a.  Annually (DoDM 5200.01-V4, Enclosure 3, Paragraph 6)
b.  Bi-annually
c.  Semi-annually
d.  Every three years
e.  Continuously

73.  Which of the following should be addressed in CUI refresher training?
a.  The importance of classified information
b.  Changes in 5200.01 V1-3
c.  Threats to DoD CUI (DoDM 5200.01-V4, Enclosure 3, Paragraph 6)
d.  B. and c.
e.  None of the above

74. Which of the following should be addressed in CUI refresher training?
   a. The importance of CUI
   b. Changes in 5200.01 V4
   c. Threats to DoD CUI
   d. B. and c.
   e. All of the above (DoDM 5200.01-V4, Enclosure 3, Paragraph 6)

75. Who should receive security management and oversight briefings?
   a. All employees
   b. Security managers
   c. Classification management officers
   d. B. and c.
   e. All of the above (DoDM 5200.01-V3, Enclosure 5 Paragraph 10)

76. Which elements should be part of a security termination briefing?
   a. Reporting unauthorized attempts to access classified information
   b. Responsibility to submit writings for security review
   c. Emphasize responsibility to protect classified information
   d. Responsibility to protect CUI
   e. All of the above (DoDM 5200.01-V4, Enclosure 3, Paragraph 9)

77. How might a cleared contractor mark unclassified training material to simulate SECRET?
   a. Unclassified Sample
   b. Secret For Training Purposes
   c. Secret For Training Only
   d. Unclassified – Classified Markings for Training Purposes Only (DoDM 5200.01-V2, Enclosure 3, Paragraph 22)
   e. All of the above

78. Initial Security Briefings should include which of the following?
   a. Define classified information
   b. Define CUI
   c. Produce a basic understanding of security principles
   d. A. and c.
   e. e. All of the above (DoDM 5200.01-V3, Enclosure 5, Paragraph 3)

79. All of the following are portion markings that one might find on foreign classified information EXCEPT:
   a. TOP SECRET
   b. SECRET
   c. REGISTERED (DoDM 5200.01-V2, Enclosure 3, Paragraph 6)
   d. RESTRICTED or In Confidence
   e. UNCLASSIFIED

80. TOP SECRET material shall be stored in:
   a. GSA approved security container
   b. Approved vault
   c. Approved open storage area with supplemental controls
   d. A. and c.
   e. All of the above (DoDM 5200.01-V2, Enclosure 3, Paragraph 6)

81. Refresher security training for cleared employees must be completed at least:
   a. Every six months
   b. Annually (DoDM 5200.01 Vol 3, Enclosure 5, Paragraph 7)
   c. Quarterly
   d. Every three months
   e. Upon discretion of FSO

82. Which of the following are part of "DoD Components"?
    a. Department of Justice
    b. FBI
    c. CIA
    d. Combatant Commands (DoDM 5200.01-V1, Enclosure 4, Paragraph 5)
    e. All of the above

83. How often are employees who conduct derivative classification required to receive derivative classifier training:
    a. Annually
    b. Semiannually
    c. Every two years (DoDM 5200.01 Vol 3, Glossary)
    d. Once
    e. On a case-by-case basis

84. Which is not a responsibility of USD(I&S) concerning advising the Secretary of Defense on the DoD Insider Threat Program?
    a. Provide oversight of the DoD Insider Threat Program.
    b. Assign responsibilities to the DoD Components to implement the DoD Insider Threat Program.
    c. Recommend improvements to the Secretary of Defense on DoD insider threat activities.
    d. Integrate insider threat activities into national and local policy (DoDM 5200.01-V1, Enclosure 2, Paragraph 1)
    e. None of the above

85. Which of the below should be consulted concerning to access to RD, FRD, and CNWDI within the DoD?
    a. NISPOM
    b. DoDM 5200.01
    c. DoDI 5200.44
    d. DoDI 5210.02 (DoDM 5200.01-V1, Enclosure 3, Paragraph 13)
    e. DoDI 5000.83

86. Critical Nuclear Weapon Design Information is a _____
category of SECRET Restricted Data or TOP SECRET Restricted Data.
    a.   DOE
    b.   DoD (DoDM 5200.01 Vol 1, Enclosure 3, Paragraph 13)
    c.   NRC
    d.   CSA
    e.   DOT

TEST 3 ANSWERS-LONG VERSION

1. What is the scope of the DoD Information Security Program?
a. Implements References (b), (d), and (f) with regard to the classification only
b. Implements References (c), (e), and (g) with regard to the declassification only
c. Implements References (b), (d), and (f) with regard to the classification, declassification, and protection of classified information (DoDM 5200.01 Vol 1, Enclosure 3)
d. Implements References (c), (e), and (g) with regard to the classification, declassification, and protection of classified information
e. Implements References (c), (e), and (g) with regard to the implementation of cybersecurity

2. Which of the following is the retention policy for controlled unclassified information?
a. Shall be maintained only when it is required for effective and efficient operation of the organization
b. Shall be maintained if law requires its retention
c. Shall be maintained if treaty requires its retention
d. Shall be maintained if international agreement requires its retention
e. All of the above (DoDM 5200.01 Vol 1, Enclosure 3, Paragraph 14)

3. Which classification considerations are associated with information released through the Freedom of Information Act (FOIA)?
a. There are none as FOIA overrides classification
b. Classified information is exempt from FOIA processes
c. The OCA should provide a description of damage with consideration to any FOIA request (DoDM 5200.01 Vol 1, Enclosure 3, Paragraph 13)
d. A. and c.
e. A. and b.

4. Of the following, which SAP control markings are optional?
   a. Level of classification
   b. Special Access Required
   c. Program nickname
   d. Code word
   e. Dissemination control (DoDM 5200.01-V2, Enclosure 4, Paragraph 7)

5. Which classification considerations are associated with non-government research and development information?
   a. The government activity shall issue guidance when protection under classification system is requested
   b. The government must determine whether or not those conducting the R&D effort have clearances
   c. If individuals conducting R&D refuse security clearances then the information may not be classified
   d. All of the above (DoDM 5200.01 Vol 1, Enclosure 4, Paragraph 19)
   e. b and d

6. Which of the following are not true about need to know?
   a. An official determination for blanket access to all classified information for a lawful and authorized governmental function
   b. All government employees have need to know
   c. All program managers have need to know of all aspects of their project
   d. Determined primarily by rank and position
   e. All of the above (DoDM 5200.01 Vol 1, Definitions)

7. What is the definition of access pertaining to protecting classified information?
   a. The right to access classified information
   b. The desire to access classified information
   c. The acceptance of classified information
   d. The opportunity to access classified information (DoDM 5200.01 Vol 1, Definitions)

e.  All of the above

8.  Which of the following are identified as authorities for declassification?
   a.  Supervisory officials of the OCA if granted authority
   b.  Officials designated by DoD component heads
   c.  NSA/CSS
   d.  A. and c.
   e.  All of the above (DoDM 5200.01 Vol 1, Enclosure 3, Paragraph 13)

9.  What are the requirements for protecting CNWDI?
   a.  Can be emailed to anyone with the appropriate clearance and need to know
   b.  Can be emailed to only those who have clearances, need to know and received additional briefings (DoDM 5200.01 Vol 1, Enclosure 3, Paragraph 13)
   c.  CNWDI information does not require password protection
   d.  Systems containing CNWDI do not need certification
   e.  A. and c.

10. Which policies are referred to for protecting SAP information?
   a.  Reference (q)
   b.  Reference (at)
   c.  DoDM 5200.01-V1
   d.  B. and c.
   e.  All of the above (DoDM 5200.01 Vol 1, Enclosure 3, Paragraph 13)

11. What are tetragraphs?
   a.  Used to identify country names
   b.  Used to identify international organizations
   c.  Used to identify international alliances
   d.  B. and c. (DoDM 5200.01 Vol 2, Enclosure 3, Paragraph 5)
   e.  All of the above

172 SFPC Master Exam Prep

12. Which is correct concerning the use of NOFORN?
    a. Must be used with HCS
    b. Must be used with TK-GEOCAP
    c. Should be reserved for Intelligence documents only (DoDM 5200.01-V2, Enclosure 4, Paragraph 6)
    d. A. and b.
    e. All of the above (DoDM 5200.01-V2, Enclosure 4 Paragraph 6)

13. Which of the following are authorized dissemination markings?
    a. FOR SHOW
    b. FOR DISPLAY
    c. CONTROLLED INFORMATION
    d. NOT AUTHORIZED FOR RELEASE
    e. DISPLAY ONLY (DoDM 5200.01 Vol 2, Enclosure 4, Fig 25)

14. Which are the requirements for protecting open storage classified materials at the TOP SECRET level?
    a. A senior official determines that security in depth is provided
    b. A cleared employee will inspect area during four hour periods
    c. An IDS response team should arrive within 30 minutes of alarm
    d. All of the above
    e. None of the above (DoDM 5200.01 Vol 3, Enclosure 3, Paragraph 3)

15. Which is not an access requirement for Secret?
    a. Non-disclosure agreement
    b. Confidential security clearance Badge card (DoDM 5200.01 Vol 1, Enclosure 3, Paragraph 12)
    c. Need to know
    d. Secret security clearance
    e. All of the above

16. Which is a specific requirement for access to Special Access Programs (SAP)?
   a.  SCI-Non-disclosure agreement
   b.  Top Secret security clearance
   c.  Need to know
   d.  Secret security clearance
   e.  DoD-approved program indoctrination (DoDM 5200.01 Vol 1, Enclosure 3, Paragraph 12)

17. Who has the authority to originally classify information?
   a.  Prime contractor
   b.  Government employees regardless of position
   c.  Individual authorized in writing to do so (DoDM 5200.01 Vol 1, Definitions)
   d.  A. and c.
   e.  All of the above

18. Which information is not found within a Security Classification Guide?
   a.  Specific items of information to be protected
   b.  Specific classification of information
   c.  Specific reason for classification
   d.  State declassification instructions
   e.  Estimated cost of protecting classified information (DoDM 5200.01 Vol 1, Enclosure 6, Paragraph 2)

19. Which is a classification duration option for originally classified information?
   a.  A date or independently verifiable event less than 10 years from the date of original classification
   b.  A date 10 years from the date of original classification
   c.  A date 25 years from the date of original classification
   d.  A date or independently verifiable event greater than 10 and less than 25 years from the date of original classification
   e.  All of the above (DoDM 5200.01 Vol 1, Enclosure 4, Paragraph 13a)

20. Which are the authorized methods for the transmission / transportation of Secret classified information?
    a.  U.S. Postal Service standard mail
    b.  U.S. Postal Service certified mail
    c.  Commercial carrier, but no requirement for surveillance service
    d.  On U.S. ships, but no receipt or agreement is necessary
    e.  None of the above (DoDM 5200.01 Vol 3, Enclosure 4, Paragraph 3)

21. Which are general requirements governing the transfer of classified information or material to Foreign Governments?
    a.  Transfers shall be conducted through contractor to contractor channels
    b.  Letters of Agreement require detailed transfer instructions
    c.  Recipients must be designated by recipient government
    d.  A. and b.
    e.  B. and c. (DoDM 5200.01 Vol 3, Enclosure 4, Paragraph 1)

22. What are the attributes of integrity as it relates to information security?
    a.  Ensure that data remains available
    b.  Ensure that data remains trusted (DoDM 5200.01 Vol 3, Enclosure 7, Paragraph 4)
    c.  Ensure data remains unavailable to unauthorized persons
    d.  Ensure users know who they are communicating with
    e.  Loss of ability to authenticate

23. Which label is appropriate for identifying Secret information on an IT system?
    a.  SF 704
    b.  SF 705
    c.  SF 706
    d.  SF 707 (DoDM 5200.01-V2, Enclosure 2, Paragraph 4)
    e.  SF 708

24. Which purposes and basic concepts are involved in properly preparing Top Secret materials for transportation?
   a. Outer wrapper must not have individual's name
   b. Outer wrapper must not indicate classification level
   c. A briefcase may serve as an outer wrapper (DoDM 5200.01 Vol 3, Enclosure 4, Paragraph 3)
   d. Specialized shipping containers may serve as outer wrapper
   e. All of the above (DoDM 5200.01 Vol 3, Enclosure 4, Paragraph 10)

25. Which of the following is not a step in the derivative classification process?
   a. Determine if information contains classified information
   b. Derived information should be portion marked
   c. Determine the duration of classification
   d. Contact the originator of classified document or consult the explanation
   e. None of the above (DoDM 5200.01 Vol 1, Enclosure 4, Paragraph 12)

26. Which actions are authorized for hand carrying classified materials?
   a. The information is already available at the delivery address
   b. The lack of operational necessity exists
   c. There are secure communications available
   d. Arrangements have been made for security storage (DoDM 5200.01 Vol 3, Enclosure 4, Paragraph 12)
   e. All of the above

27. What is the impact of cybersecurity lapses on confidentiality?
   a. Data may not be available
   b. Data may not be trusted
   c. Data may be available to unauthorized persons (DoDM 5200.01 Vol 3, Enclosure 7, Paragraph 4)
   d. Users may not be sure of whom they are communicating with
   e. Loss of ability to authenticate

28. What is the impact of cybersecurity lapses on non-repudiation?
a. Data may not be available
b. Data may not be trusted
c. Data may be available to unauthorized persons
d. Users may not be sure of whom they are communicating with (DoDM 5200.01 Vol 3, Enclosure 7, Paragraph 4)
e. Loss of ability to authenticate

29. Which is true of system categorization?
a. Some systems may need to be categorized depending on risk level
b. Depending on risk level, some IA controls may be assigned to systems
c. IA controls are selected based upon confidentiality alone
d. A. and c.
e. None of the above (DoDM 5200.01 Vol 3, Enclosure 7, Paragraph 4)

30. Which is true of a data spill?
a. Unclassified information is introduced to a classified system
b. Unclassified information is introduced to an accredited system
c. If no unauthorized disclosure occurred, then treat as no compromise
d. Classified information is introduced to an unclassified system (DoDM 5200.01 Vol 3, Enclosure 7, Paragraph 5)
e. None of the above

31. Which is true of data spill reporting?
a. Preserve evidence
b. Contain to minimize damage
c. Evidence may be used for risk assessment
d. Evidence may be used for damage assessment
e. All of the above (DoDM 5200.01 Vol 3, Enclosure 7, Paragraph 5)

32. Which of the following are identified as minimum security requirements for non-traditional work environments?
    a. Vocal approval for use of classified material
    b. Application of single layer security
    c. Secure storage of classified material is provided (DoDM 5200.01 Vol 3, Enclosure 7, Paragraph 7)
    d. Self-validation of security review
    e. None of the above

33. Which of the following are risk management roles of the security professional in managing risks associated with new technology and equipment?
    a. Understand that technology changes frequently
    b. Data storage products are increasingly changing
    c. IT peripherals bring challenges to information security
    d. Security managers should use chain of command to recommend policy changes
    e. All of the above (DoDM 5200.01 Vol 3, Enclosure 7, Paragraph 10)

34. Which of the following is true of the proper use of social networking services?
    a. Use of social media is governed by DoDI 5200.44
    b. Use of social media is governed by DoDM 5000.02
    c. Use of social medica is governed by DoDI 8170.01 (DoDM 5200.01 Vol 3, Enclosure 7, Paragraph 11)
    d. Use of social media is governed by DoDM 8150.01
    e. Use of social media is governed by DoDI 8150.01

35. Which of the following are approved for the storage of Secret classified material?
    a. GSA approved security container
    b. In open storage with supplementary controls
    c. Same manner as with Top Secret material
    d. A. and c.
    e. All of the above (DoDM 5200.01 Vol 3, Enclosure 3, Paragraph 3)

178 SFPC Master Exam Prep

36. Which of the following are approved for the storage of confidential classified material?
   a.  Requires supplemental controls
   b.  Requires GSA approved container (DoDM 5200.01 Vol 3, Enclosure 3, Paragraph 3)
   c.  Requires GSA approved vault with supplemental controls
   d.  Requires GSA approved container with supplemental controls
   e.  B. and c.

37. Which of the following is the correct approval authority for vaults?
   a.  GCA
   b.  GSA (DoDM 5200.01 Vol 3, Enclosure 3, Paragraph 3)
   c.  CSO
   d.  CSA
   e.  GTO

38. Which of the standards are not authorized for the construction of vaults to protect classified information?
   a.  Class C (DoDM 5200.01 Vol 3, Appendix to Enclosure 3, Paragraph 1)
   b.  Class A
   c.  Class B
   d.  All of the above
   e.  None of the above

39. Which of the following do not meet standards for secure rooms?
   a.  Walls may be of temporary construction (DoDM 5200.01 Vol 3, Appendix to Enclosure 3, Paragraph 1)
   b.  Doors should be constructed of wood
   c.  Floors may be constructed of wood
   d.  Roofs may be constructed of metal panels
   e.  Ceilings may be constructed of gypsum

40. IDS consists of which of the following?

a. Intrusion and detection equipment (DoDM 5200.01 Vol 3, Appendix to Enclosure 3, Paragraph 2)

b. Intrusion and denial equipment

c. Denial and detection equipment

d. Operating forces

e. None of the above

41. Which are recognized as authorized use of biometric controls for access to a secure area?

a. Guard

b. Fingerprints (DoDM 5200.01 Vol 3, Appendix to Enclosure 3, Paragraph 3)

c. Keycard

d. Lock

e. All of the above

42. What is the scope of the DoD Information Security Program?

a. Implements References (b), (d), and (f) with regard to the classification only

b. Implements References (c), (e), and (g) with regard to the declassification only

c. Implements References (b), (d), and (f) with regard to the classification, declassification, and protection of classified information (DoDM 5200.01 Vol 1, Enclosure 3)

d. Implements References (c), (e), and (g) with regard to the classification, declassification, and protection of classified information

e. Implements References (c), (e), and (g) with regard to the implementation of cybersecurity

43. Which statement best describes a security infraction?
a. Failure to comply with security requirements
b. Security incident resulting in compromise of classified information
c. Security incident that does not constitute a violation
d. A. and c. (DoDM 5200.01 Vol 3, Enclosure 5, Paragraph 1)
e. None of the above

44. What are the characteristics of an investigation?
a. Conducted when incident cannot be resolved through inquiry
b. Conducted to determine if there is a loss of classified information
c. Conducted to determine if classified information was disclosed in an unauthorized manner
d. Conducted when a security violation where in-depth examination is required
e. All of the above (DoDM 5200.01 Vol 3, Enclosure 5, Paragraph 1)

45. When are administrative controls required?
a. When personnel controls are insufficient
b. When physical controls are insufficient
c. When technical controls are insufficient
d. A. and c.
e. All of the above (DoDM 5200.01 Vol 3, Enclosure 2, Paragraph 1)

46. Which are the requirements for protecting open storage classified materials at the TOP SECRET level?
a. A senior official determines that security in depth is provided
b. A cleared employee will inspect area during four hour periods
c. An IDS response team should arrive within 30 minutes of alarm
d. All of the above
e. None of the above (DoDM 5200.01 Vol 3, Enclosure 3, Paragraph 3)

47. Which of the following statements are most accurate as described for the destruction of classified documents/materials?

a. Burning, crosscut shredding, wet pulping, chemical decomposition, pulverizing

b. Burning, mutilating, pulverizing, chemical decomposition, wet pulping

c. Burning, wet pulping, crosscut shredding

d. Burning, crosscut shredding, mutilation, wet pulping, chemical decomposition, pulverizing (DoDM 5200.01 Vol 3, Enclosure 3, Paragraph 17)

e. Burning, crosscut shredding, wet pulping, chemical decomposition, crushing

48. Which of the following constitute a primary reason(s) to reproduce TOP SECRET documents?

a. As required by operational needs (DoDM 5200.01-V1, Enclosure 2, Paragraph 15)

b. When directed by FSO

c. When directed by CSA

d. Contract is renewed

e. All of the above

49. Which response time is correct for Top Secret open storage areas with security in depth from the time of alarm announcement?

a. Three minutes

b. Fifteen minutes (DoDM 5200.01-V3, Enclosure 3, Paragraph 3)

c. Five minutes

d. Twenty minutes

e. Thirty minutes

50. Which response time is correct for Top Secret open storage areas without security in depth from the time of alarm announcement?
   a. Three minutes
   b. Fifteen minutes
   c. Five minutes (DoDM 5200.01-V3, Enclosure 3 ,Paragraph 3)
   d. Twenty minutes
   e. Thirty minutes

51. Which is identified as the senior official responsible for the portion of the manual pertaining to DoD Information Security Program pertaining to foreign government information?
   a. DoD CIO
   b. USD
   c. Undersecretary of Defense (DoDM 5200.01-V1, Enclosure 2, Paragraph 2)
   d. DTIC
   e. WHS

52. Which is identified to direct the use of technical means to prevent unauthorized copying of classified data?
   a. DTIC
   b. WHS
   c. DoD CIO (DoDM 5200.01-V1, Enclosure 2, Paragraph 3)
   d. Undersecretary of Defense
   e. USD

53. What must a person possess prior to being granted access to classified information?
   a. Appropriate security clearance
   b. Valid security clearance
   c. Need to know
   d. Signed a non-disclosure agreement
   e. All of the above (DoDM 5200.01-V1, Enclosure 3, Paragraph 12)

54. A signed SF 312 is required for which security clearance level?
a.  Confidential
b.  Secret
c.  Top Secret
d.  B. and c.
e.  All of the above (DoDM 5200.01-V1, Enclosure 3, Paragraph 12)


55. Once signed, how long must an SF 312 be retained?
a.  10 years
b.  30 years
c.  20 years
d.  50 years (DoDM 5200.01-V1, Enclosure 3 ,Paragraph 12)
e.  Indefinitely


56. Prior to gaining access to SCI information, approved individuals must sign a _____?
a.  DA authorized SCI nondisclosure agreement
b.  DoD authorized SCI nondisclosure agreement
c.  DNI authorized SCI nondisclosure agreement (DoDM 5200.01-V1, Enclosure 3 Paragraph 12)
d.  DoE authorized SCI nondisclosure agreement
e.  None of the above


57. Prior to gaining access to SAP information, approved individuals must sign a _____?
a.  DA authorized SCI nondisclosure agreement
b.  DoD authorized SCI nondisclosure agreement (DoDM 5200.01-V1, Enclosure 3 ,Paragraph 12)
c.  DNI authorized SCI nondisclosure agreement
d.  DoE authorized SCI nondisclosure agreement
e.  None of the above

58. Which DoDM 5200.01 Volume would you research to find information about the DoD Information Security Program concerning overview, classification and declassification?

a. Volume 2
b. Volume 1 (DoDM 5200.01-V1)
c. Volume 3
d. Volume 4
e. None of the above

59. Which DoDM 5200.01 Volume would you research to find information about the DoD Information Security Program concerning protection of classified information?

a. Volume 2
b. Volume 1
c. Volume 3 (DoDM 5200.01-V3)
d. Volume 4
e. None of the above

60. Which DoDM 5200.01 Volume would you research to find information about the DoD Information Security Program concerning Controlled Unclassified Information (CUI)?

a. Volume 2
b. Volume 1
c. Volume 3
d. Volume 4 (DoDM 5200.01-V4)
e. None of the above

61. Which organization is authorized to declassify COMSEC information?

a. NSA/CSS (DoDM 5200.01-V1, Enclosure 3, Paragraph 13)
b. DNI
c. DoD
d. Heads of DoD Components
e. All of the above

62. Which of the below should be consulted concerning to distribution of RD, FRD, and CNWDI within the DoD?
    a.  DoDI 5210.02 (DoDM 5200.01-V1, Enclosure 3, Paragraph 13)
    b.  NISPOM
    c.  DoDM 5200.01
    d.  DoDI 5200.44
    e.  DoDI 5000.83

63. Employees shall acknowledge that they have been given a NATO security briefing. Signed acknowledgements shall be:
    a.  Stored
    b.  Maintained (DoDM 5200.01 Vol 1, Enclosure 3, Paragraph 12)
    c.  Shredded
    d.  Not provided
    e.  Optional

64. Which of the below should be consulted concerning access to and distribution of RD, FRD, and CNWDI within the DoD?
    a.  NISPOM
    b.  DoDM 5200.01
    c.  DoDI 5200.44
    d.  DoDI 5000.83
    e.  DoDI 5210.02 (DoDM 5200.01-V1, Enclosure 3, Paragraph 13)

65. When should CNWDI information be authorized for dissemination through e-mail?
    a.  When recipient is confirmed to have final security clearance at appropriate level
    b.  When recipient is confirmed to have need to know
    c.  When recipient is confirmed to have had the required additional security briefing
    d.  A. and b.
    e.  All of the above (DoDM 5200.01-V1, Enclosure 3, Paragraph 13)

66. When should RD information be authorized for dissemination through e-mail?

    a.  When recipient is confirmed to have final security clearance at appropriate level

    b.  When recipient is confirmed to have need to know

    c.  When recipient is confirmed to have had the required additional security briefing

    d.  A. and b. (DoDM 5200.01-V1, Enclosure 3,  Paragraph 13)

    e.  All of the above

67. What is the impact of cybersecurity lapses on non-repudiation?

    a.  Data may not be available

    b.  Data may not be trusted

    c.  Data may be available to unauthorized persons

    d.  Users may not be sure of whom they are communicating with (DoDM 5200.01 Vol 3, Enclosure 7, Paragraph 4)

    e.  Loss of ability to authenticate

68. Which DoDM 5200.01 provisions may military commanders modify as necessary during military operations?

    a.  Accountability

    b.  Transmission

    c.  Dissemination

    d.  A. and b.

    e.  All of the above (DoDM 5200.01-V1, Enclosure 3, Paragraph 16)

69. Which of the following could be subject to sanctions for violations of DoDM 5200.01?

    a.  Contractor personnel

    b.  Military personnel

    c.  Civilian personnel

    d.  B. and c. (DoDM 5200.01-V1, Enclosure 3 Paragraph 18)

    e.  All of the above

70. In which of the following situations could sanctions be imposed?
    a. Disclose classified information to unauthorized persons
    b. Classify the classification of information in violation of this Volume
    c. Continue the classification of information in violation of this Volume
    d. Create or continue a SAP contrary to the requirements of this Volume
    e. All of the above (DoDM 5200.01-V1, Enclosure 3, Paragraph 18)

71. Which is true of data spill reporting?
    a. Report to the OCA
    b. Report to the information owner
    c. Report to the responsible computer incident response organization
    d. A. and c.
    e. All of the above (DoDM 5200.01 Vol 3, Enclosure 7, Paragraph 5)

72. Which of the following are identified as minimum security requirements for non-traditional work environments?
    a. Request for a crime survey were applicable
    b. Storage of classified information can be modified according to home construction
    c. Security training for employees
    d. A. and c. (DoDM 5200.01 Vol 3, Enclosure 7, Paragraph 7)
    e. B. and c.

73. Which of the following are risk management roles of the security professional in managing risks associated with new technology and equipment?

   a.   Understand that technology changes frequently (DoDM 5200.01 Vol 3, Enclosure 7, Paragraph 10)

   b.   Data storage products rarely change

   c.   IT equipment rarely brings new challenges

   d.   Security managers aren't required to identify new risks

   e.   All of the above

74. Which of the following is true of the proper use of social networking services?

   a.   Protection of CUI is not the same as with other media

   b.   Protection of classified information is the same as with other media (DoDM 5200.01 Vol 3, Enclosure 7, Paragraph 11)

   c.   Penalties for ignoring requirements don't exist for social media

   d.   Use of social media is prohibited

   e.   Non official use of social media is the only authorized use of social media

75. Which of the following are approved for the storage of Top Secret classified material?

   a.   GSA approved security container with supplementary protection

   b.   GSA approved vault

   c.   No IDS is required if cleared employee inspect container

   d.   A. and c.

   e.   A. and b.   (DoDM 5200.01 Vol 3, Enclosure 3, Paragraph 3)

76. Which of the following is the correct approval authority for security containers?

   a.   GCA

   b.   CSA

   c.   CSO

   d.   GSA (DoDM 5200.01 Vol 3, Enclosure 3, Paragraph 3)

   e.   GTO

77. Which of the standards are authorized for the construction of vaults to protect classified information?
    a. Class C
    b. Class A
    c. Class B
    d. B. and c. (DoDM 5200.01 Vol 3, Appendix to Enclosure 3, Paragraph 1)
    e. Classes A-C

78. Which is a responsibility of the Secretary of Energy?
    a. Authority for procedures for information classified under AEA
    b. Authority over access to information classified under AEA
    c. Authority over portions pertaining to information classified as RD
    d. Authority over portions pertaining to information classified as FRD
    e. All of the above (DoDM 5200.01 Vol 1, Enclosure 5, Paragraph 12)

79. What are the construction standards for secure rooms?
    a. Walls may be of temporary construction
    b. Walls should be constructed of plaster or other acceptable material (DoDM 5200.01 Vol 3, Appendix to Enclosure 3, Paragraph 1)
    c. Floors may be of temporary construction
    d. Roofs should be of temporary construction
    e. All of the above

80. Which of the following is the purpose of intrusion detection systems?
    a. Deter unauthorized access
    b. Deny unauthorized access
    c. Detect unauthorized access (DoDM 5200.01 Vol 3, Appendix to Enclosure 3, Paragraph 2)
    d. A. and b.
    e. A. and c.

81. Which are recognized as authorized use of visual controls for access to a secure area?

   a. Employee (DoDM 5200.01 Vol 3, Appendix to Enclosure 3, Paragraph 3)

   b. Fingerprints

   c. ID badge

   d. Key

   e. All of the above

82. Contractors who paraphrase classified information are making _____ decisions:

   a. Reasons for classification

   b. Security Classification Guidance

   c. Derivative classification (DoDM 5200.01 Vol 3, Enclosure 5, Paragraph 7)

   d. Classification

   e. Classified document

83. U.S. RESTRICTED AND FORMERLY RESTRICTED Data is marked all EXCEPT:

   a. COSMIC TOP SECRET ATOMAL

   b. NATO RESTRICTED ATOMAL (DoDM 5200.01 Vol 2, Enclosure 4, Paragraph 4)

   c. NATO CONFIDENTIAL ATOMAL

   d. NATO SECRET ATOMAL

   e. None of the above

84. Which are appropriate page markings for a document classified at the SECRET level?

   a. SECRET, TOP SECRET, SENSITIVE, CONFIDENTIAL

   b. CONFIDENTIAL, SECRET, UNCLASSIFIED (DoDM 5200.01 Vol 2, Enclosure 4, Paragraph 3)

   c. CONFIDENTIAL, FOUO, TOP SECRET

   d. UNCLASSIFIED, FOUO, SENSITIVE

   e. All of the above

85. TOP SECRET control officer shall be designated to _____, _____, _____TOP SECRET information.
a. Transmit, maintain access and accountability records for, and receive (DoDM 5200.01 Vol 1, Enclosure 2, Paragraph 8)
b. Create, classify, brief, document
c. Receive, create, classify, disseminate
d. Request, assign, account, disseminate
e. Receive, transmit, classify, document

86. Pulping may only be used to destroy these kinds of products:
a. Water soluble material (DoDM 5200.01 Vol 3, Enclosure 3, Paragraph 18)
b. Metal
c. Plastic
d. Rubber
e. Computer

TEST 4 - LONG ANSWER

1.   The _____ retains authority over access to intelligence
methods and sources.
   a.   DNI (DoDM 5200.01-V1, Paragraph 2)
   b.   FBI
   c.   DCSA
   d.   CIA
   e.   SECDEF

2.   The DoD Components provide classification guidance to
licensees, _____, grantees or others who possess DoD classified
information.
   a.   TAAs
   b.   Contractors (DoDM 5200.01-V1, Enclosure 5, Paragraph 11)
   c.   Licensors
   d.   Scopers
   e.   Registrars

3.   Which of the following are part of "DoD Components"?
   a.   Combatant Commands (DoDM 5200.01-V1, Enclosure 4,
Paragraph 5)
   b.   Department of Justice
   c.   FBI
   d.   CIA
   e.   All of the above

4.   SECRET material may be reproduced in the following
scenarios, EXCEPT?
   a.   In performance of the organization's mission
   b.   In compliance of applicable statutes
   c.   Upon closure of contract (DoDM 5200.01-V3, Enclosure 2,
Paragraph 14)
   d.   In compliance of Directives
   e.   None of the above

5. Visitors to DoD Component facilities shall possess _____ and _____.

    a. Clearance, need to know (DoDM 5200.01-V3, Enclosure 2, Paragraph 7)

    b. Clearance, ID card

    c. Authorized tablet, pen

    d. VAL, authorization

    e. Clearance, authorization

6. Which of the following is correct concerning the storage of TOP SECRET material?

    a. In a GSA approved container with supplementary controls

    b. Lock must meet FF-L-2740, as long as container is in an area with security in depth

    c. In an approved vault

    d. All of the above (DoDM 5200.01-V3, Enclosure 3, Paragraph 3)

    e. None of the above

7. SECRET material shall be stored in which of the following scenarios:

    a. GSA approved security container

    b. Approved vault

    c. Open storage (Supplemental controls not necessary)

    d. A. and b. (DoDM 5200.01-V1, Enclosure 3, Paragraph 3)

    e. All of the above

8. Which of the following constitute a primary reason(s) to reproduce confidential documents?

    a. As required by operational needs (DoDM 5200.01-V1, Enclosure 2, Paragraph 15)

    b. When directed by FSO

    c. When directed by CSA

    d. Contract is renewed

    e. All of the above

9. Who determines need to know at classified meetings?
a. GCA
b. Contract monitor
c. Individual disclosing information (DoDM 5200.01-V3, Enclosure 2, Paragraph 7)
d. Visiting individuals
e. FSA

10. TOP SECRET information can be transmitted by which of the following methods within the U.S. and its territories:
a. Defense Courier Service, if authorized by GCA (DoDM 5200.01-V3, Enclosure 4, Paragraph 3)
b. A courier cleared at the SECRET level
c. By electrical means over contractor approved secured communication devices
d. By government vehicle
e. By U.S. Postal Service Registered Mail

11. SECRET information can be transmitted by which of the following means:
a. Registered mail
b. Cleared commercial carrier
c. Express mail between 50 states
d. Approved cleared contractor employees
e. All of the above (DoDM 5200.01-V3, Enclosure 4, Paragraph 3)

12. Couriers shall ensure all EXCEPT:
a. Information shall not be disclosed in public areas
b. Information remains under continuous protection
c. They possess authorization to store classified in hotel safe (DoDM 5200.01-V3, Enclosure 4, Paragraph 12)
d. Locked briefcase may serve as outer layer
e. None of the above

13. The foreign government designation of RESTRICTED should be given what level of protection in the U. S. where bilateral security agreements exist:
   a. SECRET
   b. TOP SECRET
   c. CONFIDENTIAL (DoDM 5200.01-V3, Enclosure 4, Paragraph 17)
   d. UNCLASSIFIED
   e. FOUO

14. Destruction records are required for:
   a. TOP SECRET FGI  (DoDM 5200.01-V3, Enclosure 2, Paragraph 17)
   b. SECRET
   c. CONFIDENTIAL
   d. A. and b.
   e. All of the above

15. Construction in closed areas should be built of material that:
   a. Prevents opening by magnetic pulse
   b. Prevents opening by shotgun blast
   c. Provides evidence of unauthorized access (DoDM 5200.01-V3, Enclosure 3, Appendix)
   d. Protects from bomb blasts
   e. A. and c.

16. Vents with openings greater than 96 inches and over _____ inches at smallest measurement shall be protected.
   a. 2
   b. 6 (DoDM 5200.01-V3, Enclosure 3, Appendix)
   c. 9
   d. 10
   e. 18

17. Repairs of approved containers include which of the following procedures:

    a. Damaged or altered parts are replaced with manufacturer's replacement

    b. Damaged or altered parts replaced with identical cannibalized parts

    c. Damaged or altered parts are repaired with other than approved methods if storing SECRET material under supplemental controls until October 1, 2012

    d. According to FED STD 809 (DoDM 5200.01-V3, Enclosure 3, Paragraph 14)

    e. All of the above

18. Concerning FGI markings used in U.S. documents, recommendations for the declassification of NATO classified information should be forwarded to:

    a. Originating activity

    b. CSA

    c. CISSP

    d. DoD component (DoDM 5200.01-V2, Enclosure 4, Paragraph 9)

    e. FSCC

19. Verification of a meeting, the attendee's identity is verified by official photographic identification such as:

    a. Passport

    b. Contractor ID

    c. Military ID

    d. CAC card

    e. All of the above (DoDM 5200.01-V3, Enclosure 2, Paragraph 16)

20. Which of the following meeting items must be approved by the government?
   a. Menu
   b. Seating order
   c. Announcements (DoDM 5200.01-V3, Enclosure 2, Paragraph 16)
   d. Slide show background
   e. Dress code

21. When taking action to downgrade classified information, which organization approves the action?
   a. GSA
   b. CSA
   c. OCA (DoDM 5200.01-V1, Enclosure 5, Paragraph 3)
   d. FBI
   e. CSO

22. Which of the following apply to end of day security checks?
   a. Perform checks at the close of each working day
   b. Perform checks at end of last shift in which classified material was removed for use
   c. Not necessary during continuing 24 hour operations
   d. A. and c.
   e. All of the above (DoDM 5200.01-V3, Enclosure 2, Paragraph 9)

23. Which E.O. provides information on marking classified email?
   a. E.O. 12353
   b. E.O. 13526 (DoDM 5200.01-V2, Enclosure 3, Figure 3)
   c. E.O. 11257
   d. E.O. 13691
   e. E.O. 12563

24. Which is a responsibility of the Secretary of Energy?
    a.  Authority for procedures for information classified under AEA
    b.  Authority over access to information classified under AEA
    c.  Authority over portions pertaining to information classified as RD
    d.  Authority over portions pertaining to information classified as FRD
    e.  All of the above (DoDM 5200.01-V3, Enclosure 6, Paragraph 5)

25. Which of the following should derivative classifiers accomplish?
    a.  Be an original classifier
    b.  Complete derivative classifier training (DoDM 5200.01-V3, Enclosure 5, Paragraph 7)
    c.  Complete a waiver if derivative classifier training is not available
    d.  Complete FSO certification training
    e.  A. and c.

26. Which of the following are appropriate portion markings found on classified documents?
    a.  SECRET, TOP SECRET, CONFIDENTIAL
    b.  S, TS, C (DoDM 5200.01-V3, Enclosure 3, Paragraph 6)
    c.  UNCLASSIFIED, TS, CONFIDENTIAL
    d.  FSO, TS, C, U
    e.  All of the above

27. The _____ has authority pertaining to access to intelligence methods and sources.
    a.  NSA
    b.  DoD
    c.  DNI (DoDM 5200.01-V1, Enclosure 3, Paragraph 4)
    d.  DOA
    e.  GCA

28. Contractors shall report all unauthorized disclosure concerning RD and FRD to the:
   a.  DOE
   b.  NRC
   c.  DoD Component (DoDM 5200.01-V3, Enclosure 6, Paragraph 5)
   d.  GCA
   e.  FSO

29. Challenges to improperly classified RD/FRD documents should be addressed through the:
   a.  DoD Component (DoDM 5200.01-V3, Enclosure 6, Paragraph 5)
   b.  CSA
   c.  DOE
   d.  DoD
   e.  NRC

30. Contractors shall not disclose CNWDI to subcontractors without approval of the:
   a.  CSA
   b.  DoD Component (DoDM 5200.01-V3, Enclosure 6, Paragraph 5)
   c.  DOE
   d.  NRC
   e.  FSO

31. For government sponsored classified meetings at contractor facilities, who is responsible for assuming security jurisdiction?
   a.  The cleared contractor
   b.  The subcontracted security force
   c.  Authorizing government agency (DoDM 5200.01-V3, Enclosure 2, Paragraph 16)
   d.  Proprietary guard force
   e.  CSA

32. TOP SECRET material shall be stored in a(n):
a. GSA approved security container
b. Approved vault
c. Approved closed area with supplemental controls
d. a and c
e. All of the above (DoDM 5200.01-V3, Enclosure 3, Paragraph 1)

33. Which of the following can authorize the removal of Top Secret information for use at home?.
a. Chairman of the Joint Chiefs of Staff
b. Combatant Commanders
c. Director of National Intelligence
d. Secretary of Defense
e. All of the Above (DoDM 5200.01-V3, Enclosure 2, Paragraph 12)

34. Foreign nationals can participate in classified meetings if authorized by the head of the _____ authorizing the meeting.
a. U.S. Government Agency (DoDM 5200.01-V3, Enclosure 2, Paragraph 16)
b. FSO
c. CSO
d. Contractor
e. None of the above

35. Reproduction of foreign TOP SECRET information requires approval of the:
a. GCA
b. Originating Government (DoDM 5200.01-V3, Enclosure 2, Paragraph 15)
c. CSA
d. State Department
e. None of the above

36. Employees on federal installations shall safeguard classified information according to procedures of:
    a. NISPOM
    b. Block 13 of DD Form 254
    c. Host Installation or Agency (DoDM 5200.01-V3, Enclosure 5, Paragraph 1)
    d. CSA
    e. CSO

37. Who is responsible for providing declassification guidance or notification?
    a. CSA
    b. CSO
    c. GSA
    d. Senior Government Official and OCA (DoDM 5200.01-V1, Enclosure 5, Paragraph 1)
    e. None of the above

38. The _____ is a foreign official assigned to receive classified information from the U.S. government.
    a. COR
    b. DGR (DoDM 5200.01-V1, Enclosure 4, Paragraph 5)
    c. FSO
    d. GCA
    e. State Department

39. The _____ determines when foreign nuclear information removed from the RD category can be declassified:
    a. Secretary of Energy (DoDM 5200.01-V1, Enclosure 5, Paragraph 12)
    b. DASD(NM)
    c. NRC
    d. DoD
    e. None of the above

40. The _____ determines when FRD pertaining to defense nuclear information can be declassified:
   a.  Secretary of Energy
   b.  DASD(NM) (DoDM 5200.01-V1, Enclosure 5, Paragraph 12)
   c.  NRC
   d.  DoD
   e.  None of the above

41. Which of the following constitute a primary reason(s) to reproduce SECRET documents?
   a.  As required by operational needs (DoDM 5200.01-V1, Enclosure 2, Paragraph 15)
   b.  When directed by FSO
   c.  When directed by CSA
   d.  Contract is renewed
   e.  All of the above.

42. The _____ has agency oversight for implementation of the DoD Information Security Program.
   a.  Secretary of Defense
   b.  Director of FBI
   c.  Defense Security Services
   d.  Director of ISOO (DoDM 5200.01-V1, Enclosure 3, Paragraph 5)
   e.  Cognizant Security Agency

43. Which of the following are part of "DoD Components"?
   a.  DOE
   b.  DOJ
   c.  FBI
   d.  CIA
   e.  Military Departments (DoDM 5200.01-V1, Paragraph 2)

204 SFPC Master Exam Prep

44. Which of the following are part of "DoD Components"?
a.  DOE
b.  DOJ
c.  FBI
d.  CIA
e.  Military Departments (DoDM 5200.01-V1, Paragraph 2)

45. Which of the following are part of "DoD Components"?
a.  DOE
b.  Office of the Inspector General of the Department of Defense (DoDM 5200.01-V1, Paragraph 2)
c.  DOJ
d.  FBI
e.  CIA

46. Which of the following are part of "DoD Components"?
a.  DOE
b.  DoD Field Activities (DoDM 5200.01-V1, Paragraph 2)
c.  DOJ
d.  FBI
e.  CIA

47. Which of the following are part of "DoD Components"?
a.  DOE
b.  Combatant Commands (DoDM 5200.01-V1, Paragraph 2)
c.  DOJ
d.  FBI
e.  CIA

48. Which of the following are part of "DoD Components"?
a.  DOE
b.  Office of the Chairman of the Joint Chiefs of Staff (DoDM 5200.01-V1, Paragraph 2)
c.  DOJ
d.  FBI
e.  CIA

49. Which of the following are NOT part of "DoD Components"?
a. DOE (DoDM 5200.01-V1, Paragraph 2)
b. Office of the Chairman of the Joint Chiefs of Staff
c. Combatant Commands
d. Office of the Inspector General of the Department of Defense
e. DoD Field Activities

50. Derivative Classification includes:
a. Incorporated classified information
b. Restated classified information
c. Generate classified information in a new form
d. All of the above (DoDM 5200.01-V3, Definitions)
e. B. and c.

51. Which inspection requirement is correct for Secret open storage areas with security in depth?
a. Every five hours
b. Every six hours
c. Every three hours
d. Every twenty hours
e. Every four hours (DoDM 5200.01-V3, Enclosure 3, Paragraph 3)

52. Who ensures reviews are conducted for classification challenges?
a. OCA (DoDM 5200.01-V3, Enclosure 5, Paragraph 5)
b. CSA
c. FSO
d. FBI
e. GSA

SFPC Master Exam Prep

53. Required security training and briefing titles for all cleared employees include:

    a.   Initial orientation and annual refresher training (DoDM 5200.01-V3, Enclosure 5, Paragraph 10)

    b.   OCA training and annual awareness training

    c.   Declassification training and annual refresher training

    d.   OCA training and annual refresher training

    e.   Initial security briefings, annual, refresher


54. All classified information and material should be marked to clearly convey:

    a.   Level of classification

    b.   Portions that contain classified

    c.   Declassification instructions

    d.   Date of origin

    e.   All of the above (DoDM 5200.01-V2, Enclosure 3, Paragraph 3)


55. NATO has the following identified levels of security classification EXCEPT:

    a.   COSMIC TOP SECRET

    b.   NATO SECRET

    c.   NATO CONFIDENTIAL

    d.   NATO RESTRICTED

    e.   NATO TOP SECRET (DoDM 5200.01-V2, Enclosure 4, Paragraph 4)


56. CONFIDENTIAL is approved for transmission by which of the following means?

    a.   U.S. Postal Service Priority Mail

    b.   U.S. Postal Service First Class Mail

    c.   Any commercial overnight delivery company

    d.   U.S. Postal Service Certified Mail (DoDM 5200.01-V3, Enclosure 4, Paragraph 5)

    e.   All of the above

57. Authorization in writing by the _____ is required for transmission of classified information to a foreign government.
   a. CSA
   b. CSA
   c. FSO
   d. CSA
   e. DSA (DoDM 5200.01-V3, Enclosure 4, Paragraph 5)


58. What should be used as authorization to approve a courier in DD Form 2501?
   a. Identification of an individual's recurrent need to hand-carry
   b. Signature of an appropriate official
   c. Emergency communication procedures
   d. a and b (DoDM 5200.01-V3, Enclosure 4, Paragraph 13)
   e. a. and c.


59. Which government agency has jurisdiction over RD?
   a. NSA
   b. FRD
   c. DNI
   d. CSA
   e. DOE (DoDM 5200.01-V3, Enclosure 6, Paragraph 5)


60. Working papers shall be marked the same as finished documents and at the same classification level. Which answer is correct concerning initial draft date?
   a. Transmitted within the facility
   b. Retained for more than 30 days from creation
   c. Retained for more than 180 days from creation (DoDM 5200.01-V1, Enclosure 4, Paragraph 9)
   d. Retained for more than 120 days from creation
   e. Retained for more than 130 days from creation

61. Classified material may be destroyed by which of the following methods?
   a. Mutilation
   b. Chemical decomposition
   c. Pulverization
   d. Melting
   e. All of the above (DoDM 5200.01-V3, Enclosure 3, Paragraph 15)

62. Need to know is generally based on:
   a. Level of clearance
   b. Block 13 of DD Form 254
   c. Security Classification Guide
   d. Authorized government function (DoDM 5200.01-V3, Glossary)
   e. As determined by CSA

63. Which of the following apply to end of day security checks?
   a. Perform checks at the close of each working day
   b. Perform checks at end of last shift in which classified material was removed for use
   c. Not necessary during continuing 24 hour operations
   d. A. and c.
   e. All of the above (DoDM 5200.01-V3, Enclosure 2, Paragraph 9)

64. What should organizations ensure their derivative classifiers accomplish?
   a. Be an original classifier
   b. Complete derivative classifier training (DoDM 5200.01-V3, Enclosure 5, Paragraph 7)
   c. Complete a waiver if derivative classifier training is not available
   d. Complete FSO certification training
   e. A. and c.

65. Alternative Compensatory Control Measures include items identified as classified:
    a.  SECRET
    b.  CONFIDENTIAL
    c.  Intelligence (DoDM 5200.01-V2, Enclosure 4, Paragraph 11)
    d.  TOP SECRET
    e.  None of the above

66. _____ is a DoD category of TOP SECRET Restricted Data or SECRET Restricted Data that reveals operation of components of a thermonuclear bomb.
    a.  CNWDI (DoDM 5200.01-V2, Enclosure 4, Paragraph 11)
    b.  FRD
    c.  RD
    d.  NATO
    e.  EWNDI

67. Water soluble papers shall be destroyed by:
    a.  Shredding
    b.  Burning
    c.  Disintegration
    d.  Pulping (DoDM 5200.01-V3, Enclosure 3, Paragraph 18)
    e.  A. b. and c.

68. How shall employees certify that they have received a NATO security briefing?
    a.  Orally
    b.  Verbally (DoDM 5200.01-V1, Enclosure 3, Paragraph 12)
    c.  No acknowledgement is required
    d.  No briefing is required
    e.  A. and b.

69. Which response time is correct for Secret open storage areas with security in depth from the time of alarm announcement?
    a. Three minutes
    b. Fifteen minutes
    c. Five minutes
    d. Twenty minutes
    e. Thirty minutes (DoDM 5200.01-V3, Enclosure 3, Paragraph 3)

70. Which E.O. covers Classified National Security Information?
    a. E.O. 12353
    b. E.O. 13526 (DoDM 5200.01-V2, Enclosure 1, References)
    c. E.O. 11257
    d. E.O. 13691
    e. E.O. 12563

71. Which agency has classification authority of COMSEC information?
    a. NSA (DoDM 5200.01-V2, Enclosure 1, References)
    b. DIA
    c. CIA
    d. DoD
    e. DOE

72. The _____ provides the security classification guides.
    a. FSO
    b. CSA
    c. OCA (DoDM 5200.01-V3, Enclosure 5, Paragraph 3)
    d. DoD
    e. Secretary of Defense

73. The SF 312 must be maintained for how long?
    a. Two years
    b. Twenty years
    c. Eighteen months
    d. Fifty years (DoDM 5200.01-V1, Enclosure 3, Paragraph 12)
    e. Five years

74. Methods of approved refresher training include:
a. Briefings
b. Instructional materials
c. Videos
d. A. and c.
e. All of the above (DoDM 5200.01-V3, Enclosure 5, Paragraph 8)


75. Freight forwarders who take custody of classified material must have:
a. FCL
b. Adequate space
c. Proper security level storage capacity
d. A. and b.
e. A. and c. (DoDM 5200.01-V3, Enclosure 4, Paragraph 7)


76. TOP SECRET information can be transmitted by which methods:
a. Direct contact between appropriately cleared persons (DoDM 5200.01-V3, Enclosure 4, Paragraph 3)
b. Registered mail
c. Express mail
d. Carriers listed under NISP
e. U.S. government contract vehicles


77. TOP SECRET information can be transmitted by which methods:
a. DCS
b. Authorized U.S. government agency courier services
c. Direct contact between appropriately cleared persons
d. Electronic means over an approved secure communications system
e. All of the above (DoDM 5200.01-V3, Enclosure 4, Paragraph 3)

78. Which DoD Instruction covers the dissemination of CNWDI?
    a. DoDI 5210.02 (DoDM 5200.01-V3, Enclosure 4, Paragraph 3)
    b. DoDI 5200.44
    c. DoDI 5200.39
    d. DoDI 5205.11
    e. None of the above

79. When is a signed receipt required for transmission of CONFIDENTIAL material?
    a. Only when transmitted on U.S. registry ships (DoDM 5200.01-V3, Enclosure 4, Paragraph 5)
    b. Always a requirement
    c. If receipt has errors
    d. A. and c.
    e. All of the above

80. Which label is appropriate for identifying Top Secret information on an IT system?
    a. SF 704
    b. SF 705
    c. SF 706 (DoDM 5200.01-V2, Enclosure 2, Paragraph 4)
    d. SF 707
    e. SF 708

81. Information classified as SECRET can be transmitted outside of facility by all means EXCEPT:
    a. Defense Courier Service, if authorized by GCA
    b. U.S. Postal Service Registered Mail
    c. U.S. Postal Service Priority Mail (DoDM 5200.01-V3, Enclosure 4, Paragraph 4)
    d. Cleared commercial carrier
    e. Cleared commercial messenger service

82. When wrapping classified material for shipment, the _____ cannot go on the outer label:
   a. Classification level (DoDM 5200.01-V3, Enclosure 4, Paragraph 10)
   b. Office code letter
   c. Office code number
   d. Directions for routing
   e. Facility name

83. All of the following must be included in the authorization letter for hand carrying classified material on a commercial aircraft EXCEPT:
   a. Traveler's Social Security Number (DoDM 5200.01-V3, Enclosure 4, Paragraph 14)
   b. Full name of individual
   c. Name of person designated to confirm courier authorization
   d. Courier card including date of issue and expiration
   e. Name of official issuing letter

84. Which E.O. provides information on marking classified email?
   a. E.O. 12353
   b. E.O. 13526 (DoDM 5200.01-V2, Enclosure 4, Paragraph 3)
   c. E.O. 11257
   d. E.O. 13691
   e. E.O. 12563

85. Which best explains the retention policy for classified and controlled unclassified information?
   a. Shall be maintained only when it is required for effective and efficient operation of the organization
   b. Shall be maintained if a law requires its retention
   c. Shall be maintained if a treaty requires its retention
   d. Shall be maintained if an international agreement requires its retention
   e. All of the above (DoDM 5200.01 Vol 1 Enclosure 3, Paragraph 14)

86. Which cover sheet is appropriate for Confidential information?
   a.  SF 701
   b.  SF 702
   c.  SF 703
   d.  SF 704
   e.  SF 705 (DoDM 5200.01-V2, Enclosure 2, Paragraph 4)

## TEST 1 SHORT VERSION

| | | |
|---|---|---|
| 1. a | 34. d | 67. e |
| 2. e | 35. c | 68. e |
| 3. e | 36. e | 69. a |
| 4. c | 37. c | 70. e |
| 5. e | 38. e | 71. d |
| 6. d | 39. d | 72. e |
| 7. b | 40. b | 73. b |
| 8. d | 41. e | 74. c |
| 9. a | 42. d | 75. d |
| 10. e | 43. e | 76. d |
| 11. e | 44. e | 77. e |
| 12. b | 45. e | 78. c |
| 13. c | 46. e | 79. b |
| 14. c | 47. a | 80. b |
| 15. c | 48. a | 81. a |
| 16. e | 49. e | 82. d |
| 17. e | 50. a | 83. d |
| 18. d | 51. e | 84. c |
| 19. d | 52. a | 85. d |
| 20. e | 53. d | 86. b |
| 21. d | 54. c | |
| 22. a | 55. d | |
| 23. a | 56. d | |
| 24. a | 57. b | |
| 25. b | 58. b | |
| 26. c | 59. d | |
| 27. e | 60. d | |
| 28. a | 61. a | |
| 29. a | 62. e | |
| 30. c | 63. e | |
| 31. e | 64. e | |
| 32. e | 65. e | |
| 33. b | 66. e | |

## TEST 2 SHORT VERSION

| | | |
|---|---|---|
| 1. b | 35. b | 69. e |
| 2. e | 36. b | 70. c |
| 3. a | 37. c | 71. e |
| 4. b | 38. e | 72. a |
| 5. e | 39. e | 73. c |
| 6. c | 40. e | 74. e |
| 7. a | 41. e | 75. e |
| 8. d | 42. e | 76. e |
| 9. d | 43. d | 77. d |
| 10. d | 44. d | 78. e |
| 11. a | 45. c | 79. c |
| 12. e | 46. e | 80. e |
| 13. b | 47. e | 81. b |
| 14. c | 48. d | 82. d |
| 15. d | 49. e | 83. c |
| 16. b | 50. e | 84. d |
| 17. d | 51. e | 85. d |
| 18. e | 52. e | 86. b |
| 19. a | 53. e | |
| 20. e | 54. c | |
| 21. e | 55. c | |
| 22. e | 56. a | |
| 23. c | 57. e | |
| 24. e | 58. c | |
| 25. c | 59. e | |
| 26. b | 60. b | |
| 27. a | 61. e | |
| 28. d | 62. e | |
| 29. d | 63. e | |
| 30. d | 64. a | |
| 31. d | 65. a | |
| 32. d | 66. e | |
| 33. e | 67. e | |
| 34. e | 68. e | |

# *TEST 3 SHORT VERSION*

1. c
2. e
3. c
4. e
5. d
6. e
7. d
8. e
9. b
10. e
11. d
12. c
13. e
14. e
15. b
16. e
17. c
18. e
19. e
20. e
21. e
22. b
23. d
24. c
25. e
26. d
27. c
28. d
29. e
30. d
31. e
32. c
33. e

34. c
35. e
36. b
37. b
38. a
39. a
40. a
41. b
42. c
43. d
44. e
45. e
46. e
47. d
48. a
49. b
50. c
51. c
52. c
53. e
54. e
55. d
56. c
57. b
58. b
59. c
60. d
61. a
62. a
63. b
64. e
65. e
66. d

67. d
68. e
69. d
70. e
71. e
72. d
73. a
74. b
75. e
76. d
77. d
78. e
79. b
80. c
81. a
82. c
83. b
84. b
85. a
86. a

# TEST 4 SHORT VERSION

| | | |
|---|---|---|
| 1. a | 34. a | 67. d |
| 2. b | 35. b | 68. e |
| 3. a | 36. c | 69. e |
| 4. c | 37. d | 70. b |
| 5. a | 38. b | 71. a |
| 6. d | 39. a | 72. c |
| 7. d | 40. b | 73. d |
| 8. a | 41. a | 74. e |
| 9. c | 42. d | 75. e |
| 10. a | 43. e | 76. a |
| 11. e | 44. e | 77. e |
| 12. c | 45. b | 78. a |
| 13. c | 46. b | 79. a |
| 14. a | 47. b | 80. c |
| 15. c | 48. b | 81. c |
| 16. b | 49. a | 82. a |
| 17. d | 50. d | 83. a |
| 18. d | 51. e | 84. b |
| 19. e | 52. a | 85. e |
| 20. c | 53. a | 86. e |
| 21. c | 54. e | |
| 22. e | 55. e | |
| 23. b | 56. d | |
| 24. e | 57. e | |
| 25. b | 58. d | |
| 26. b | 59. e | |
| 27. c | 60. c | |
| 28. c | 61. e | |
| 29. a | 62. d | |
| 30. b | 63. e | |
| 31. c | 64. b | |
| 32. e | 65. c | |
| 33. e | 66. a | |

# WHAT NEXT?

Perhaps at this time you are re-reading this chapter having become certified. You may be wondering what to do next. There is certainly more work to do as industrial security requirements continue to evolve. Current events have demonstrated this need for change as the security manager implements new technologies and devices and new certifications become available. I would recommend that you continue to engage with training, teaching, studying and growing. This will be necessary in maintaining your certifications. I encourage you to continue to improve your grasp of not only protecting our nation's assets, but protecting your employees and your product.

I also recommend taking additional certifications such as the Industrial Security Professional (ISP®) or ISOC. We have study aids for those exams as well. These study aids also could be used to earn education credits for recertification.

An industrial security professional or security specialist may understand the process of requesting clearance actions, filing security paperwork, accounting for classified materials, building closed areas and performing per the Contract Security Classification Specification, DD Form 254. However, an industrial security manager should also understand physical security, insider threat, prevention of workplace violence, risk analysis and security surveys, business continuity and physical security and IT convergence.

The security professional has other non-DoD resources available to improve their comprehension of the total job description. There are other certifications including the Certified Protection Professional (CPP) from ASIS International. Additional certifications and the study to earn those certifications increase the security professional's understanding of security. Along the way, they will learn tools to address security issues with corporate executives, present return on investment of security expenditures and create metrics for security effectiveness.

Thank you for continuing to develop your skills as an industrial security professional. We would also like to thank you for all you do to protect our way of life and guard our Nation's secrets. Our desire is that this book has encouraged your professional growth. If you have enjoyed this book, please feel free to leave a review as we want to hear your comments. Feel free to contact me using my website: www.redbikepublishing.com. I would also invite you to continue your studies with my books, *How to Get U.S. Government Contracts and Classified Work* and *Insider's Guide to Security Clearances*, as they make the perfect study companions. Also, consider browsing our other books before your next job interview; it will help increase your knowledge and awareness of security requirements and skills. We also invite you to download and study our NISPOM training. You can find training and other resources at www.redbikepublishing.com and https://www.bennettinstitute.com.

# CONCLUSION

This concludes our book and I hope you have found it informative and useful. I also hope that I have delivered on my promise of helping you prepare to take the SFPC certification exam.

## ABOUT THE AUTHOR

 Jeffrey W. Bennett, ISOC, ISP®, SAPPC, SFPC is a security expert with experience in the Army, U.S. Government and as a Facility Security Officer (FSO). He consults on security issues full time with his other company, Thrive Analysis Group, Inc at www.thriveanalysis.com.

Jeff is enthusiastic about protecting our nation's secrets. He believes that integrity, influence and credibility are paramount qualities required of security professionals. His primary goal is to show cleared defense contractors and government program offices how to bring about security awareness, build influence within the organization and to make a difference where they work.

He speaks, writes, consults and provides products to help professionals better protect sensitive and classified information. Jeff is the author of many books including: *How to Get U.S. Government Contracts and Classified Work, Insider's Guide to Security Clearances, The Side Job Tool Box* and several novels.

Jeff is available to conduct on site SPeD and ISP certification training, NISPOM training, program protection training and more. Contact him below for more information.

**Contact Jeff:**
editor@redbikepublishing.com
Hear Jeff's Podcast at:
*https://www.redbikepublishing.com/dodsecure*

If you want an in-depth review of NISPOM (section by section) and DoDM 5200.01, we have training at:
*https://bennettinstitute.com.*

**Red Bike Publishing**
Our company is registered as a government contractor company with the CCR and VetBiz (DUNS 826859691). Specifically we are a Service Disabled Veteran Owned Small Business. Red Bike Publishing provides high quality books and training @
www.redbikepublishing.com.

## Books

This book, other security and NISP books and training are also available at our website. Helpful books include those part of the Security Clearances and Cleared Defense Contractor series by Red Bike Publishing:

- Insider's Guide to Security Clearances
- How to Get U.S. Government Contracts and Classified Work
- National Industrial Security Program Operating Manual (NISPOM)
- Self Inspection Guidebook for NISP Contractors
- International Traffic In Arms Regulation (ITAR)

## Training

Training topics include the follow either stand alone or as an FSO Certification Bundle https://www.redbikepublishing.com/fsocertification/:

- SF-312 Non Disclosure Briefing
- Insider Threat Training
- Derivative Classifier Training
- Security Awareness Training

Bennett Institute https://www.bennettinstitute.com

NISPOM Fundamentals Course-Training that discusses each chapter of the NISPOM in depth; more than 8 hours of recorded training

- Alternatively, you can take course one chapter or topic at a time
- Great study material. Each course provides completion certificates that can be used to earn CEUs for recertification.
- We also have a complimentary course available called Certification Test Tips

### A special word of thanks and a favor to ask

Thank you for buying my book. I really appreciate you being a reader and hope you find it helpful. If you have any questions, please feel free to contact me.

I would really love to hear your feedback and your input would help to make the next version of this book and my future books better. Please leave a helpful review, where you purchased your book, of what you thought of it.

I would also ask that you let a friend know about the book as well. Thanks so much and best of success to you!!

Jeffrey W. Bennett

Sign up for our reader newsletter:
*https://www.redbikepublishing.com/contact*


For more information on cleared defense contracting, security clearances, and training, check out our video.
*https://www.redbikepublishing.com/security/*

Made in United States
Orlando, FL
28 September 2023

37390894R00124